What's
Bugging
You?

Arthur V. Evans

What's Bugging You?

A Fond Look at the
Animals We Love to Hate

University of Virginia Press
Charlottesville and London

University of Virginia Press

© 2008 by the Rector and Visitors of the University of Virginia

Printed in the United States of America on acid-free paper

First published 2008

9 8 7 6 5 4 3 2 1

LIBRARY OF CONGRESS CATALOGING-IN-PUBLICATION DATA

Evans, Arthur V.

What's bugging you? : a fond look at the animals we love to hate / Arthur V. Evans.

p.   cm.

Includes bibliographical references and index.

ISBN 978-0-8139-2698-8 (cloth : alk. paper)

1. Insects—Virginia—Popular works. 2. Insect pests—Virginia— Popular works. 3. Evans, Arthur V. I. Title.

QL467.E92 2008

595.7—dc22   2007022666

These columns were originally published in abbreviated form in Arthur V. Evans's column What's Bugging You? in the *Richmond Times-Dispatch.*

Illustrations by Graham H. Wilson: Greenhouse stone cricket, 2; Damselfly, 32; Luna moth, 52; Eastern Hercules beetle, 70; Paper wasp, 90; Periodical cicada, 108

Contents

Acknowledgments

I wish to extend my heartfelt thanks to my editor at the *Richmond Times-Dispatch,* Pauline Clay. Not everyone has the curiosity, foresight, and courage to help establish and encourage a monthly newspaper column on insects and spiders. She continues to give me free rein in my column—What's Bugging You?—to write about whatever insects, spiders, and their relatives that capture my curiosity.

I am especially grateful to the many *Times-Dispatch* readers who took the time to write to me and ask questions, share experiences, or just to say hello and offer a word of thanks and encouragement. Thanks to the digital age, several people have sent vacation photos of insects and spiders from the field for me to identify or just for the sake of sharing. Although I cannot respond to everyone's messages, I do very much appreciate each and every note and image.

I am particularly indebted to my editor at the University of Virginia Press, Boyd Zenner. A fellow bug nut, her unflagging enthusiasm and unstinting support made this book possible. As a result, our professional relationship has evolved into a warm and wonderful friendship.

Special thanks to Jennifer Ackerman for allowing me to use the quote from her book *Notes from the Shore.* I found this book to be an inspiration on so many levels and am very pleased to include the short excerpt from it here in the epilogue.

My friends, neighbors, and colleagues in Virginia and beyond have helped to keep my perspective on insects and spiders fresh. They have provided me with plenty of grist for the mill, supplying me with a seemingly endless supply of specimens and questions, many of which have inspired these essays. Seeing the world of these small, yet amazing animals through their eyes has helped enormously to reacquaint me with species long forgotten or to draw my attention to aspects of their lives heretofore overlooked. There are too many of you to list here, but I trust that in one way or another, each of you knows who you are. I am very fortunate and honored to have all of you in my life.

The topic of insects and spiders is so vast that it is impossible to be an expert on all of their lives. Therefore, a book such as this is really a collaborative effort, with many all-too-often unsung collaborators, both living and not. The information presented here is a distillation of books, as well as articles gleaned from dozens of disparate scientific journals. Thanks to my own extensive entomological library; the libraries of the National Museum of Natural History, Smithsonian Institution, Washington, D.C.; the University of Richmond, Richmond, Virginia; and the World Wide Web, the basic information needed to generate the substantive prose in most of my essays was nearly always at my fingertips.

Most of all, I am thankful to my wife, Paula. It was she who first suggested that I write something for the *Richmond-Times Dispatch* in May 2000, starting with an article featuring the scarlet red and black boxelder bugs that had just begun amassing on fences and tree trunks in our neighborhood. She critically reads each and every draft of my essays before I send them off to the *Times-Dispatch,* a process that spares me the indignity of numerous typographical errors and missing words that unfortunately typify my attempts to edit my own work. She has taught me much about writing for a popular audience in a clear and engaging manner. Her love, support, and curiosity about nature continue to inform and inspire me.

What's
Bugging
You?

Prologue

My fascination with insects began when I was five years old, living on the fringes of the Mojave Desert in southern California. By the time I had entered the first grade, insect books fueled my growing interest. *An Ant Is Born,* by Harald Doering, captured my imagination with its detailed photographs of the castes and life cycles of ants. Herbert Zim's *Golden Guide to Insects* filled my head with images of various insects from across the country, including several in this book. *The Bug Club: A Handbook for Young Bug Collectors,* by Gladys Conklin, became my call to arms. I was totally captivated by the idea of exploring the tiny, alien world in my own backyard. I soon began to organize neighborhood bug safaris for my friends, my first foray into public insect education. I knew right then and there that I wanted to be an entomologist when I grew up.

My desire to learn more about insects has led me all over the western United States, especially southeastern Arizona, as well as Mexico and southern Africa. After a twelve-year stint as the director of the Insect Zoo at the Natural History Museum of Los Angeles County, I packed up and moved to Richmond, Virginia, in January 2000. It was like starting all over again. The insects and spiders living on the East Coast were different, yet familiar. To my surprise there were few popular publications on insects and spiders living in the commonwealth. Instead, I had to rely on information retrieved from mostly articles in widely scattered scientific publications. Pest information abounded in books and on the World Wide Web, but there was little in the way of basic information on nonpest species that make up the vast majority of insects that cross our paths in the commonwealth everyday. My course as a writer and photographer was set.

1

Home and

Garden

Bestiaries

Anyone who has been camping knows that the great outdoors is literally crawling with insects and spiders. The same can be said for our homes and gardens, too, where these amazing creatures seem to appear out of nowhere, uninvited and, more often than not, unwelcome. But their presence is not always accidental. Many of them purposely invade our homes to take advantage of our bountiful resources. And why shouldn't they?

As a result, minute black or brown beetles and their larvae enter our cupboards to munch their way into boxes of rice or other stored grains. Tiny pale caterpillars wander into our pantries, entangling cereals, nuts, and dried fruits with their delicate webbing, metamorphosing into drab gray moths that flit about our homes. Columns of ants march with impunity across our counters, walls, and floors, carting off fats, sweets, and water with equal enthusiasm. After dark, cockroaches emerge from their lairs in the darkest recesses of our homes to take full advantage of our inadvertent largesse left in pet dishes, trash cans, or untidy kitchens.

Down below, out of sight and usually out of mind, dozens, sometimes hundreds of large, leggy crickets lurk inside our garages, sheds, and basements in search of food and mates. Where do they all come from? How did they get in? It is as if our personal efforts at homeland security—for example, doors, windows, vents, and screens—meant nothing to them at all. Well, simply put, they don't.

Outdoors, insects are constantly assaulting carefully tended plants in hard-won gardens. Plants, or parts thereof, are sucked, drained, nibbled, chewed, skeletonized, or removed outright. What is going on? These six-legged mowers, pruners, and pumps behave as though all our hard work in the garden was simply a means for setting up a veritable buffet just for them. And soon the predators move in to take advantage of this insect hubbub. Spiders cast their webs far and wide to snag some of this bounty; their webs festoon windows, blanket lawns, and coat shrubs. Curiously, nature's most efficient insect predators are considered by many people to be a downright nuisance. Just think how many bugs there would be without these hungry arachnids!

To be sure, there are things that can and should be done to reduce the presence of animals we consider pests and minimize their impact on our belongings. But the most practical and cost-effective method is often one that simply involves a shift in perception. It's called tolerance. Instead of treating every perceived trespass as an assault that must be met with an overwhelming show of toxic force, why not embrace these encounters as an opportunity to marvel at and understand, at relatively close range, some of the most amazing animals that share our planet? After all, these uninvited creatures living in our midst are just doing what comes naturally—what they have done over countless millennia. Insects and spiders have clearly learned to adapt to us; isn't it time that we use our big brains and opposable thumbs to learn to adapt to them?

Urban Assault Beetles
and Other Pantry Pests

Was your summer and fall plagued with tiny beetles in your cereal? Do pale, slender moths flit about your television screen at night? Winter is the time to start thinking about a thorough and directed spring-cleaning to rid your home of these annoying and uninvited insect guests.

Beetles, moths, and other insects have long nibbled on scattered seeds and grains, or scavenged rotting fruits and decaying flesh in the wild. The moment we arrived on the scene and began to store and process these very same materials for our own purposes, these six-legged opportunists were quick to exploit this vast new and concentrated resource.

These tiny munchers quickly adapted to living in our food stores, becoming unwelcome pests. Many are now cosmopolitan, residing in factories, mills, warehouses, grocery stores, and pantries around the world, dispersed by commerce and other human activities.

Their small size, usually 5 mm or less, allows them to fly undetected into buildings from outside sources such as nearby rodent, bird, or insect nests. They also hitchhike into our homes on old furniture, rugs, drapes, bedding, and other materials of plant or animal origin.

Some beetles can be particularly irksome. Confused flour beetles, *Tribolium confusum,* closely resemble another beetle pest (hence the confusion is ours, not theirs). One of the most important pests of stored foods in supermarkets and homes, they ravage legumes, shelled nuts, dried fruits, spices, chocolate, even drugs and museum specimens. The rice weevil, *Sitophilus oryzae,* is a pest of stored cereals, especially, as you might expect, rice. Its cousin, the grain weevil, *Sitophilus granarius,* prefers wheat and barley products. The bane of cigar aficionados everywhere, the cigarette beetle, *Lasioderma serricorne,* not only eats tobacco, it also attacks spices, legumes, grains, and cereal products. Another pest, the drugstore beetle, *Stegobium paniceum* eats all of the above, plus herbs, biscuits, and candy for good measure.

Indian mealmoths, *Plodia interpunctella,* are so named because their larvae feed on coarsely ground grains, such as cornmeal, aka Indian meal. The larvae attack crackers, biscuits, dried fruits, nuts, and pet food, to name just a few. As they nibble, the larvae spoil the food by laying down unappetizing sheets of silken webs. At maturity, the whitish larvae migrate up the walls and cupboards to pupate, spinning their cocoons where the walls and ceilings meet.

Many pantry pests live and breed in the organic debris that inevitably accumulates on pantry shelves and cupboard corners. Periodic and thorough cleaning of these and other harborage sites will reduce numbers of pests or eliminate them altogether, eliminating the need for pesticides.

Avoid storing foods for long periods by purchasing smaller quantities that can be used quickly. Unused and uninfested materials must be stored in sealed tins or heavy plastic containers with tight-fitting lids to thwart pest infestations.

Carefully inspect any and all packages of cereal, dried food, nuts, flour, meal, pasta, chocolate, cocoa, soup mixes, spices, dry pet foods, and bird seed. Place suspect items in a clear, sealed plastic bag for later examination to determine if there is pest activity. When in doubt, throw it out! But don't worry. Accidentally ingested pantry pests don't spread disease, they simply add a little extra protein to your diet, along with an oh-so-delicate crunch.

To find out more about household insect pests and their identification and control, visit http://everest.ento.vt.edu/Facilities/OnCampus/IDLab/Fact/Fact3.html.

Letter from an Insect Gardener

With the arrival of the first warm days of the year, many Virginians, including myself, begin to scratch about in their gardens. But my interest in gardening is not rooted in a love of plants; it comes from a completely different direction. I plant a garden that attracts insects.

Butterfly gardens are a familiar sight these days at schools, parks, botanical gardens, and zoos. But these gardens are usually stocked only with flowers that provide nectar for butterflies. Why not grow plants that will also sustain their caterpillars, as well as other insects and spiders?

During the summer drought of 2002, all life seemed to shrink and coalesce along the banks of rivers and streams, or along pond edges. Well-stocked and diverse gardens became important oases for wildlife, especially birds and insects.

For example, the butterfly gardens at Holton School here in Richmond and at Three Lakes Nature Center and Aquarium in Henrico County became magnets for arthropods during the drought. Their fresh, bright blooms not only lured butterflies but also attracted other fascinating insects and spiders from the withering vegetation nearby. These gardens had become a microcosm for an amazing diversity of multilegged creatures that somehow manage to eke out a living in residential areas and business parks all too often cluttered with sterile lawns and other nonnative plantings.

The riot of insect life that assembled in these gardens inspired me to create my own insect "hot spot" right at home. If done correctly, my insect garden would not only become a haven to butterflies, bugs, beetles, and dragonflies, but it would also relieve my wife and me of a significant chunk of our useless lawn, along with all the maintenance that goes with it.

In late 2002, I staked out a piece of land that would become my insect paradise. I cautiously peeled away the thatch of grass, careful to leave behind all the invertebrate soil dwellers already in residence, especially earthworms. The fallen leaves of autumn were then mixed into the soil as the first layer of mulch. It felt good to recycle this annual accumulation of plant material rather than just raking it into the gutter to be gobbled up by the city's street sweepers.

Throughout the winter, all of our rinds, peels, cores, and other vegetable cuttings were buried or spread about the plot. The decomposition of these plant materials loads the soil with precious nutrients needed to sustain what I hoped would be a careful selection of mostly native insect-attractant plants.

I suppose now is the time for a true confession. I am not now, nor will I ever be, a gardener. I just don't have the time or patience. When I tell my neighbors that the plants in my garden are simply a necessary evil to attract insects, I am not kidding!

Fortunately for me, a good friend and neighbor is a professional landscape designer. For more than twenty years, Jacquie Gooding has designed and planted gardens that actually encourage and sustain local wildlife, including insects. Armed with my information on caterpillar and beetle food plants and her knowledge of nectar plants for bees and butterflies, we set off to a local nursery in Mechanicsville that sells varieties of native plants.

At the nursery we climbed into a golf cart and tooled up and down the rows of potted plants, selecting one of those, two of these, and four of them. In relatively short order, pots of coreopsis, goldenrod, joe-pye weed, milkweed, salvia, and scabiosa, as well as numerous small herbs all found their way onto the cart. Although not native to the area, a couple of butterfly bushes were added to the mix to juice up the selection and guarantee a steady parade of butterflies, moths, bees, beetles, and wasps through the garden.

I also purchased a wide variety of plants known to appeal to all stages of insects. I picked up a few varieties of tomatoes in an effort to attract one of my favorite insects, the three-inch-long, green, sausage-shaped caterpillar known to all as the tomato hornworm. Honeysuckle is a favorite food plant of the caterpillars of hummingbird moths. Caterpillars of the black swallowtail favor fennel plants. And milkweeds would provide sustenance not only for monarch caterpillars but also the brightly colored large milkweed bugs and milkweed beetles.

The plants were set in the ground with a handful of peat and a pinch or two of nutrients to give them a bit of a boost right out of the pot. I then covered the soil with a mixture of half pine and half hardwood mulch. The woody chips not only hold in moisture, slow rampant weed growth, and add even more nutrients to the soil, but they also provide shelter for all kinds of crickets, millipedes, spiders, and other ground-dwelling arthropods.

I added a small pond, complete with a babbling waterfall. Not wanting to add to Richmond's already burgeoning mosquito population, I seeded the pond with few adult water scorpions and dragonfly larvae that I collected in a nearby pond. The voracious appetites of these predators kept my pond free of mosquito larvae throughout the entire season. At first I was concerned that they would not have enough to eat, but I found that an endless supply of hapless insects trapped on the pond's surface created a round-the-clock buffet for my mosquito-control team.

With a trickling waterfall, mud bank, flat, bare rocks, and a selection of plants whose blooming periods overlapped throughout the spring, summer, and fall, my insect garden was good to go. Throughout the year we were treated to a colorful procession of insects and spiders. In spring and summer, female carpenter and mining bees packed their legs with pollen, while dragonflies, such as white-tailed skimmers, basked on the rocks.

Later in the season, monarchs flitted through the garden to sip butterfly bush nectar and lay their eggs on the milkweed. By the end of summer, several generations of black swallowtails had found food, shelter, and a place to pupate among the low rambling growth.

The insect garden also became an outdoor classroom of sorts, drawing both curious neighbors and fascinated children. All were treated to impromptu lessons in insect reproduction, development, mimicry, and camouflage.

This year I plan to expand my garden by adding a few more insect-friendly microhabitats, such as a clay bank for mud daubers and potter wasps and old bits of wood and other plant materials to provide the basic ingredients for paper wasps to build their nests. The possibilities for attracting new insects and spiders to my garden are endless.

For a list of butterfly-friendly plants, visit http://www.ext.vt.edu/departments/envirohort/factsheets2/specdesigns/jul88pr1.html.

Insects We Love to Hate:
Greenhouse Stone Crickets

While moving bags of potting soil on the front porch, I discovered a gathering of variously sized leggy and very nervous creatures. Their pale bodies, reaching nearly ¾ of an inch in length, appeared to be brown banded, supported by long legs mottled with patches of gray and rust. Their long, hairlike antennae waved nervously about as I knelt down for a closer look. At first glance, they looked decidedly spidery in appearance. They scampered easily up, over, and around vertical surfaces of concrete, brick, and paneling and quickly disappeared into the nearby shrubbery. I had stumbled upon a congregation of camel crickets known as greenhouse stone crickets, *Tachycines asynamorus.*

The name *Tachycines* is derived from a combination of Greek words meaning "fast and ash-colored." The specific epithet *asyn-*

amorous is Latin and means "without love," possibly a reference to our decided inability to embrace this interesting member of the insect order Orthoptera (a group that includes grasshoppers, crickets, and katydids).

Greenhouse stone crickets are distinguished from other camel crickets in Virginia by their preference for urban surroundings and a pair of small, closely set horns located between the antennae. Their long antennae—which may exceed three times the body length—combined with long legs, may fool some people into thinking they are spiders.

Their powerful jumping legs can launch them up to four feet in the air. Mature females have a long, swordlike egg-laying tube, or ovipositor, which they use to place up to several hundred eggs in the soil. The eggs are laid in spring and take about two or three months to hatch. The young, wingless crickets, or nymphs, strongly resemble the adults but are smaller in size. Adults live for about a year. Greenhouse stone crickets overwinter either as nymphs or adults.

Greenhouse stone crickets are commonly called camel crickets. Camel and cave crickets are so named because of their humpbacked appearance. As a group, they have a decided fondness for living in caves, crevices, hollow trees, and basements, or under logs and stones. They are strictly nocturnal, venturing out during the day only when disturbed. Without wings or other sound-producing structures, camel crickets are silent, never contributing to the evening chorus. Some species are thought to drum their abdomens on the soil in an effort to attract mates.

Some of the two hundred or so species of camel and cave crickets known to occur in North America originally hail from other parts of the world. An immigrant from China, the greenhouse stone cricket first became established in the warm, moist greenhouses of Europe and North America, and is now cosmopolitan.

During heavy rains or hot, dry days, greenhouse stone crickets will invade garages, sheds, and basements, often assembling by the dozens or hundreds. Indoors, the crickets are attracted to areas that are dark and humid, such as bathrooms and laundry rooms. Clothing and linens stored in these areas may be damaged if persistent populations of greenhouse stone crickets cannot find suitable plant food nearby.

Outdoors, greenhouse stone crickets are commonly found on the ground, beneath stones and logs, or in piles of firewood. Areas overgrown with ivy and other ground covers provide excellent hiding places for them. They feed on living plants and small insects. In greenhouses, seedlings, flowers, seeds, or young leaves may be eaten, but the damage is seldom serious. They will also scavenge other plant and animal materials.

There are several simple, yet effective environmental controls to reduce or prevent the invasion of unwanted crickets, including:

1. caulking or sealing window frames, doors and vents
2. installing weather stripping along the bottom of the house and garage doors
3. improving ventilation in crawl spaces and attics to reduce moisture
4. keeping ground cover, shrubs, and mulch away from the foundation
5. stacking firewood away from the house
6. removing clutter found around the home that attracts unwanted insects.

As you read this, you can take comfort in the fact that right now, in your basement or elsewhere on your property, these sociable little creatures are taking refuge. Whether we like it or not, our steady supplies of food and water, served up in artificially warmed and hydrated environments, have made it possible for greenhouse stone crickets to be a regular part of our lives.

To find out more about camel crickets and their control, visit http://www.ces.ncsu.edu/depts/ent/notes/Urban/camelcrickets.htm.

A Bounty of
Boxelder Bugs

As an entomologist, I am often asked about insects and what, if anything, should be done about them. A neighbor sought my advice regarding tiny, scarlet, mitelike creatures scurrying across his deck and up his walls. Some of these insects, no larger than coarsely ground pepper, had found their way into his home, where they congregated in the well-lit windows on the south side of the house. Armed with my insect field guide and a hand lens, I inspected his property and confirmed my suspicions; they were just boxelder bugs.

For the past few weeks, I had noticed congregations of adults and nymphs sunning themselves along the alleys and roadsides. I assured my neighbor that they posed no threat to property or pets and only in large numbers might they cause damage to some plants.

Boxelder bugs have strawlike mouth parts used to pierce plant tissues and suck out fluid nourishment. Upon hatching from the egg, the young bugs, or nymphs, resemble small, wingless versions of the adults. They undergo a series of growth stages, each punctuated by the complete shedding of their rigid external skeleton. The final adult stage marks the end of growth and is characterized by the complete development of two pairs of wings. The forewings are thickened near the body and are thin and membranous at the tips. When the wings are folded flat over their back at rest, the resulting pattern often resembles the letter x.

Adult boxelder bugs are flat, dark-gray insects with three red lines behind the head and may reach ½ inch in length. The thickened portions of their wings are bordered with red, while the membranous tips are blackish. They are strong fliers, flashing their bright red abdomens when they spread their wings and take to the air. Young nymphs are mostly red in color, but later stages appear darker as their wing pads grow larger. Both adults and nymphs have long, thin antennae.

Hibernating adults leave their winter hideaways with the advent of warm weather in late March or early April. Soon the females begin laying their dark reddish eggs in the crevices of bark on box elder trees and other nearby objects. The eggs hatch in two or three weeks, just as succulent new box elder leaves are beginning to appear. The nymphs eat and grow, shedding their external skeleton five times before becoming a fully winged adult. There are one to two generations of boxelder bugs produced each year.

Both adults and nymphs prefer the seed-bearing female box elder trees, sucking sap from the new leaves, tender twigs, and developing seeds. They also attack other trees, such as ash and maple, plum, cherry, apple, and peach, as well as grapevines and strawberries. Damage from their feeding activities may cause blotchy yellow patches or brown spots on fruit and leaves. Severe infestations of boxelder bugs can cause misshapen leaves and fruit, but mature and healthy plants rarely suffer permanent harm.

In the late spring and early fall, flying or crawling boxelder bugs begin converging on stone piles, tree holes, and other protected places, sometimes by the hundreds. They sometimes invade buildings, crowding into cracks and crevices in walls, door and window casings, and around foundations. They do not bite, nor do they damage buildings, furnishings, clothing, or food. However, they can spot curtains and walls with their waste and will leave a stain if crushed.

The best way to keep unwanted boxelder bugs, as well as other insects and spiders, out of your house is by improving home security. Replace screens and door sweeps. Repair thresholds and secure pet doors. Screen vents and other openings. Caulk and seal all possible entry sites near doors, windows, crawl spaces, light fixtures, utility pipes or wires, weather boarding, and in areas along the foundation.

For boxelder bugs already in the house, vacuuming, sweeping, or picking them up are the most effective methods for dispatching them. They do not feed on household structures or reproduce indoors so there is no need to use chemical controls inside the home. Aerosol sprays designed to kill ants and cockroaches are generally ineffective against boxelder bugs.

Outdoors, large populations of boxelder bugs can be reduced by removing leaf litter and other debris that serve as egg-laying sites near the base of female (seed-producing) box elder trees. Other hiding places, such as piles of boards, rocks, leaves, grass, and other debris close to the house, should be removed. Remove plant materials away from the house. For example, rake leaves and grass away from the foundation, especially on the south and west sides of the structure. Since boxelder bugs prefer to feed and lay their eggs on female box elder trees, plant male box elder trees instead. Male trees, propagated from cuttings taken from other male trees, may be purchased from the nursery. These measures will reduce the numbers of boxelder bugs looking to get inside your warm and cozy home.

As with many other insects labeled as "pests," a little knowledge of their habits can help to reduce costly and sometimes unnecessary reliance upon pesticides, while at the same time raising our levels of tolerance and wonder. To me, the recent appearance of boxelder bugs is just another marvelous pulse in the seasonal cycle of life. I am not the only one who feels this way. Just ask the folks in Minneota, Minnesota. They celebrate these little creatures each year with Boxelder Bug Days, a fall festival featuring bug races, bug poetry, plays, and other activities. If you can't beat 'em, join 'em!

To learn more about boxelder bugs and their control, visit http://www.ext.vt.edu/departments/entomology/factsheets/ boxelder.html.

Reintroducing the Earwig

One of the more familiar inhabitants of moist gardens and woods are the earwigs. The name "earwig" is derived from the old European superstition that these insects purposely crawl into the ears of sleeping persons. Earwigs do like to hide in small, dark places, so it is not unlikely that earwigs have, from time to time, taken refuge in a warm, dark ear, but no more so than other insects seeking safety.

Curiously, earwigs were prescribed for persons suffering from hearing disorders during medieval times. A concoction known as "oil of earwigs" was made from their dried and pulverized bodies blended with the urine of a hare and applied to the ear.

They are all too often thought to be a bane to homeowners and gardeners, who consider them to be nuisances because of their mere presence, or outright pests because they occasionally nibble on valued plants in gardens and greenhouses. But earwigs are not what they seem. Read on.

Omnivorous gourmands, earwigs consume mosses, lichens, and algae, as well as the occasional flower petal mixed with a grain or two of pollen. Some are known to invade hives and dine on the hard-earned honey of bees. As predators and scavengers, earwigs devour insects, spiders, and mites, dead or alive.

They move about at night to search for food, hiding by day in moist, dark, tight-fitting places under stones, logs, or bark, or deep inside flowers. Some species are quite gregarious, living in groups of dozens or hundreds of individuals. Though seldom noticed aloft, many earwigs are capable of flight and take to the air on bright, sunny days or warm nights, when they are frequently drawn to lights.

The long, flat, flexible bodies of earwigs come in various shades of brown or black. At one end is an antlike head, while the other bears distinctive pincerlike forceps. The forceps of both males and females are used for defense, capturing prey, and courtship. They also assist in the delicate process of folding and unfolding their fan-shaped wings beneath short, leathery wing covers. When handled, earwigs will attempt to use their forceps as pincers, but they are quite harmless.

About 1,350 species of earwigs are known worldwide, with most species living in the tropics. Of the twenty-two species of earwigs found in North America, more than half were introduced from Europe and the tropics. Seventeen species are known to live east of the Mississippi, many of which are known to occur in Virginia.

The cosmopolitan European earwig, *Forficula auricularia,* is dark reddish-brown. Its head and wing covers are distinctly reddish, while the legs and antennae are pale yellow. Adults reach nearly ½ inch or more in length. They are found throughout the United States and southern Canada and are well known to gardeners for their tendency to feed on the cultivated plants. But they are also partially predatory and eat aphids, ant eggs, and caterpillars.

The striped earwig, *Labidura riparia*, is a tropical species common in the southern United States, Arizona, and southern California. Its nearly ½-inch body is pale brown or chestnut, with distinct black markings. They prefer to eat flies and other small insects and are effective predators of some moth caterpillars that infest lawns. They will turn their attention to plants when animal food is scarce but rarely achieve the pest status of the European earwig. Striped earwigs are sometimes attracted to lights and, when entering homes in large numbers, are considered a nuisance.

Adult ring-legged earwigs, *Euborellia annulipes,* appear to be native to North America. They are wingless with a dark brown body supported by pale yellow legs marked with distinct or faint rings. A cosmopolitan species, ring-legged earwigs are most common along the coast. They are sometimes a pest in greenhouses and nurseries and may become a nuisance by invading homes, especially in the Gulf states. However, they are also known to prey on leafhoppers, beetles, moths, and some stored-grain pests.

Some earwigs guard and care for their eggs and young. The female first digs a chamber in the soil or litter to lay batches of smooth, oval eggs that are pearly white, yellowish, or cream-colored. She frequently turns and licks the eggs to keep them moist and free of mold. The eggs hatch in as little as eight days in warmer climates. Young earwigs often remain in the chamber where the mother feeds them regurgitated food. They undergo from four to six molts before reaching maturity. One or two generations are produced annually.

The giant, or St. Helena earwig, *Labidura herculeana,* is the world's largest earwig. Their bodies range from two to three inches in length, including the forceps. These wingless giants were first described in 1798, but were lost to science until their rediscovery on the South Atlantic Island of St. Helena in 1965. Forty giant earwigs, the last ever seen alive, were collected between 1965 and 1967 by a Belgian team of scientists who considered them locally abundant. They have not been seen alive since.

A few Asian and African earwigs are parasitic. They lack well-developed pinchers and their claws are especially adapted for clinging to the hair of free-tailed bats and giant pouched rats, where they feed on skin, hair, and fungus. Unlike other earwigs, parasitic ear-wigs do not lay eggs but bear live young. Because of their unusual behavior and body modifications, some scientists consider them to be somewhat distant relatives of the garden-variety earwig.

Earwigs are attacked and eaten by ants, beetles, grasshoppers, crickets, centipedes, spiders, lizards, and birds, while some flies and nematode worms are internal parasites. To defend them-selves, most earwigs use their powerful forceps as a menacing pinching weapon. Some species have abdominal glands capable of spraying noxious defensive fluids at threats three or four inches away. Earwigs are also quick on their feet, capable of scurrying away at speeds of up to four inches per second.

Earwigs that invade homes in large numbers are often consid-ered household pests in the Gulf states and southern California, but they are really only more of a nuisance since their numbers far outweigh any damage they cause. By simply sealing and screen-ing vents, repairing or adjusting door sweeps, and removing ivy and other ground-cover plants growing up against foundations, the flow of ground-dwelling insects and spiders moving through a home can be reduced significantly.

Earwigs may be abundant in moist, healthy gardens. Although they occasionally cause damage to flowers and seedlings, their mere presence should not be cause for alarm. In spite of their reputations as pests, the main economic impact of earwigs in and around the home is the time and money wasted in trying to con-trol them with needless applications of pesticides.

To learn more about earwigs, see http://tolweb.org/tree?group =Dermaptera&contgroup=Neoptera.

For more information on earwigs and their control, visit http://www.ext.vt.edu/departments/entomology/factsheets/earwigs.html.

Roly-Polies: Pillbugs and Sowbugs

Roly-polies, or wood lice, are common and familiar animals be-neath rocks and in leaf litter. They are known by many names, such as pillbugs, sowbugs, and potatobugs. Solitary pillbugs are often seen strolling about on warm spring and summer evenings. Sowbugs are sometimes encountered in large congregations under the peeling bark of standing stumps. All of these curious animals make their livings as scavengers, nibbling algae, fungi, moss, bark, and decaying plant and animal tissues. Wood lice are occasionally considered nuisances by gardeners and commercial growers when they attack mushrooms, seedlings, fruit, and other cultivated plants.

In spite of their small size and numerous legs, pillbugs and sowbugs are not really "bugs" at all. They are crustaceans and are related to lobsters, crayfish, crabs, shrimp, and barnacles. They are classified as isopods, a name that means "equal foot." This refers to the similar size and shape of all fourteen of their walking legs. Most of the world's four thousand species of isopods are marine, living as scavengers, borers, or parasites on fish and other sea animals.

Wood lice are one of the few groups of crustaceans that are truly adapted for life on land. Their close relatives, known as slaters, are very similar in appearance, live along rocky coastal shores, and are a bit more amphibious, figuratively keeping one foot on land and the other in the ocean.

The flattened, tanklike bodies of these prehistoric-looking animals are formed by a series of overlapping armored plates. Some pillbugs roll up into a ball, like an armadillo, presenting ants and other predators with a nearly impenetrable defense. Sowbugs can only curl their bodies.

The head bears the eyes and two pairs of antennae, one larger and one smaller. The short abdomen is protected on its underside in both marine and terrestrial species by pairs of flattened leglike structures called pleopods. The pleopods serve as breathing devices, while the last abdominal segment is tipped with a pair of leglike structures called uropods, which take up moisture and dispose of waste products.

In spite of their decidedly terrestrial existence, wood lice must maintain a film of moisture over their pleopods to breathe. They conserve moisture by becoming active at night to take advantage of the increased relative humidity, and by seeking dark, moist places during the day. Water is taken up at both ends, either by drinking or absorption through the uropods. Wood lice rid themselves of excess water and waste gases by exposing their porous bodies to the circulating night air. This is why they sometimes climb up on walls and trees at night after heavy rains.

Unlike terrestrial crabs that must return to the sea to reproduce, female wood lice carry their water with them in a brood pouch called the marsupium. After hatching, up to one hundred young remain in the fluid-filled marsupium for several days until they are ready to strike out on their own. Wood lice take about a year to mature and may live up to three years or more.

Several diseases infect wood lice, leaving them literally a bit blue. Individuals appearing bright blue or purple in color are infected by an iridovirus, a viral disease that infects only terrestrial invertebrates. The blue color is caused by light reflected from viral bodies produced by the virus. Birds, reptiles, amphibians, spiders, harvestmen, mites, centipedes, flies, and nematode worms also attack wood lice.

About one hundred species of wood lice inhabit in the United States and Canada, several of which were accidentally introduced from Europe. Two of the most common wood lice found in and around homes and gardens in Virginia are the common pillbug, *Armadillidium vulgare,* and the sowbug, *Porcellio scaber,* both originally from Europe.

Fifteen of Virginia's indigenous isopod species are considered uncommon to extremely rare, living only in caves or subterranean freshwater systems. The fragility of these ecosystems makes these crustaceans extremely susceptible to environmental disturbances.

In fact, two Virginia species benefit from federal protection. The endangered Lee County isopod, *Lirceus usdagalum,* was known only from four caves located in south central Lee County. The species was wiped out in one of the caves in the late 1980s as a result of sawmill activity at the cave's sinkhole entrance. Since then, a few additional specimens have been collected from two nearby springs, apparently washed out from subterranean water systems. The threatened Madison Cave isopod, *Antrolana lira,* is an extremely rare species that lacks both eyes and pigment. It is known only from deep groundwater lakes in two caves in southeastern Augusta County.

Wood lice are fascinating creatures and are seldom of any economic consequence to humans. But if wood lice do become a nuisance, the simplest and most effective method is simply to eliminate the ever-damp environments that draw in these moisture-loving animals like magnets. Excess watering around piles of plant materials or ground-hugging plants, such as ivy, creates an environment especially attractive to wood lice; it's the isopod equivalent to throwing out the welcome mat.

But why try to control or get rid of pillbugs and sowbugs? Why not learn to enjoy their presence and marvel at how they have adapted from a life at sea to that on land? I say live and let live!

Magnificent
Mantids

The end of summer is marked by a flurry of insect activity, especially around flowers. Bees, butterflies, wasps, and others dart and flit among the last blooms of the season, imbibing nectar and gathering pollen before their sources dry up, wither, and die.

Often perched discreetly among this late-season buffet is the green and brown Chinese mantid, *Tenodera aridifolia.* These rapacious predators became established on both coasts of North America in the late 1890s. The larger, heavier-bodied females can measure in at a whopping four inches in length. Both males and females are equipped with front legs bristling with rows of sharp spines that can lash out with deadly speed and accuracy, clamping down on unsuspecting insect prey like a vice. Chinese mantids eat all kinds of insects with ease and can even overpower stinging bees and wasps.

With their own time running out, female Chinese mantids must quickly acquire enough protein to ensure that the hundreds of eggs already bulging within her abdomen will develop properly. Once her appetite is slaked, she injects up to two hundred eggs into a protective foamy mass. When attached to a plant stem, the mass soon hardens, surrounding the eggs in a round, tough papery case about one inch in diameter that will see them through the winter.

Thousands of these brown, styrofoamlike egg cases find their way into hardware stores and nurseries each spring, where they are sold as biological-control agents. Gardeners intent on using fewer pesticides and boosting existing populations of beneficial predators purchase the cases and place them in their gardens to hatch. Like their parents, hungry mantid hatchlings feed opportunistically, eating any insect they can catch, including their siblings. They do not have the same value system as we do and will make meals out of both beneficial and pest species.

Mantids are classified in the order Mantodea and are closely related to grasshoppers, crickets, cockroaches, and stick insects. About 1,800 species of mantids are known worldwide, most of which live in the tropics. About twenty species—native and introduced—are known from the United States and Canada.

The name "mantis" is derived from an ancient Greek word that means prophet or soothsayer. When not in use, the mantid's prominent front legs are held folded in front of its body, suggesting the act of prayer and giving rise to the common name "praying mantis."

Male mantids are often smaller than females, sometimes only half their size. Depending on the species, the wings of females are sometimes shorter and are often more colorful and less transparent than those of the males.

As adults, many mantid species have a single ear located in the middle of the thorax near its junction with the abdomen. They are able to hear the ultrasonic echolocation signals used by bats to detect flying insect prey. Upon hearing such signals while in the air, night-flying mantids roll sharply and enter into a spiral dive to dodge the bats, increasing their speed as they drop to the ground or seek refuge inside shrubs or other protective vegetation.

The next time you are out in the garden or walking along a park hedgerow, take some time to inspect the lush vegetation just below the conspicuous blooms and riot of insect activity hurtling about them. There somewhere, lurking in the shadows and tangles, you are likely to find a well-camouflaged mantid or two, picking off this year's pollinators and converting them into next year's predators.

For pictures and more information about praying mantids, visit http://bugguide.net/node/view/176.

Cockroaches 101:
A Primer

For all you cockroach-phobes out there, it's time to turn off your gag-o-meters, stifle your sense of disgust and indignation, sit back, take a deep breath, and read on. I think that you will be surprised and fascinated by these oft-maligned creatures, most of which are not pests.

Did you know that cockroaches scavenge plant and animal tissues and recycle their nutrients for future use by other organisms? Some cockroaches are even thought to be important pollinators. Countless animals around the world, including humans, depend on their protein-rich bodies for food. And the Chinese use them to treat all kinds of maladies, while their study in the laboratory helped to launch a relatively new field of medicine, neuroendocrinology.

But for most of us, cockroaches are just bad news. At best, they are a social stigma and at worst, a persistent and unyielding infestation. Just walk through any grocery or hardware store and you will come across shelf after shelf of brightly colored aerosol cans filled with lethal toxins, each formulated to mete out death to a particular kind of cockroach. And, for the same price, you can take out some ants, fleas, and hapless spiders, too.

Parents of small children and pet owners wisely opt for more directed control methods, choosing bait stations and sticky traps to rid their abodes of unwanted guests. Yet, in spite of every effort to exclude them from our homes, cockroaches keep coming back for more. Why?

Certain kinds of cockroaches live with us because they have the same basic requirements we do. They need water all the time. They like warm, stable temperatures. And they always like to have plenty of food around. As far as some cockroaches are concerned, our thermostat settings, dietary requirements, and waste-management systems—or lack thereof—make living with us a much better bet than taking their chances in nature. Along with other household "pests," they make their living by simply taking advantage of the resources that we leave behind.

Left to their own devices, cockroaches will build up huge populations in homes, businesses, and sewers. They often congregate in large numbers during the day behind cabinets, inside wall spaces, and beneath floorboards, venturing out at night to feed. The smell of a large cockroach infestation is pungent and unmistakable.

Cockroaches eat almost anything, both plant and animal in origin. They will even make a meal out of cooking-oil film that settles in the kitchen, or the dander that flakes off you and your pets. Some pest species can survive up to three months without food, but most will die in just days without water.

The bodies of pest cockroaches, both inside and out, teem with fungi, bacteria, parasitic worms, and other microscopic organisms. Still, there is no direct evidence that cockroaches spread diseases among humans. Regardless of the conditions they live under, cockroaches are incredibly fastidious animals and spend a considerable amount of time grooming themselves. They pay special attention to their sensitive antennae and bristly feet.

In spite of their personal hygiene, the mere presence of cockroaches in a home or business can trigger allergic reactions among people who are especially sensitive. Over time, scientists and technicians regularly working with cockroaches may eventually experience allergy attacks, asthma, or skin irritations when exposed to their research subjects or to materials that have come in contact with them.

Homeowners can drastically reduce the size of cockroach infestations simply by tidying up. Repair leaky pipes and faucets. Don't leave pet food and water dishes out overnight, inside or out. Don't leave dirty dishes in the sink and take out the garbage every night before going to bed. Remove stacks of newspapers, magazines, and shopping bags, as these provide uninvited guests with plenty of harborage sites. And make sure garbage cans outside have tight-fitting lids.

Apartment dwellers will have a tougher time since the efficacy of these measures requires all tenants to cooperate simultaneously with the same degree of enthusiasm and efficiency. Persistent infestations may require the expertise of licensed exterminators, but the fruits of their efforts are prolonged only when combined with consistently good housekeeping.

There are about four thousand species of cockroaches worldwide, but only about twenty different kinds of these are considered pests. In Virginia, the most familiar cockroaches were introduced from somewhere else. The large, brown American cockroach is actually from West Africa. The shiny, dark Oriental cockroach, or water bug, is slightly smaller and originally hails from Asia. They bubble up periodically from tub drains, or stroll with impunity down city sidewalks on warm humid nights. The smaller, pale German cockroach is also an Asian import.

Not all human interactions with cockroaches are negative. Pest species are commonly used as study animals for all kinds of scientific research. Engineers have developed tiny robots using cockroaches as models. Equipped with wristwatch-sized sensors and video cameras, these "biobots" are able to "see" and take measurements in remote places unsafe for humans, such as buildings that have been destroyed by bombs or earthquakes. In parts of Asia, humans regularly eat cockroaches as food. In southern China and in Chinatowns across America, dried cockroaches are sold for medicinal purposes. And big and beefy Madagascan hissing cockroaches are bred and kept in captivity as unusual pets.

The vast majority of cockroaches live in the wet, humid tropics, but some prefer the mountains or deserts. About seventy different kinds, mostly nonpests, live in the United States and Canada. These "wild" cockroaches live almost everywhere except in extremely cold habitats. However, one species does manage to eke out a living on the slopes of Mount Everest, some three and a half miles above sea level. Virginia's native species prefer to live their lives in the dark recesses of caves and animal burrows, or under bark, logs, stones, or dead leaves.

Most North American species are uniformly black, brown, or reddish brown. But some tropical species have distinctive markings that warn potential predators of their distastefulness. Some brightly colored cockroaches mimic bad-tasting fireflies and ladybugs, or even stinging wasps. Although we know volumes about cockroaches that regularly live with us, very little is known about species that prefer to live in more pristine environments.

Most cockroaches put their eggs in a pillowlike capsule and leave it somewhere, never to see their young. But one Virginia species, the brown-hooded wood cockroach, *Cryptocerus punctulatus*, is an exception. One of the most primitive cockroaches in the world, this species lives more like a termite than a cockroach, chewing tunnels and galleries in rotten wood. Males and females mate for life and raise their young in families that stay together three or four years.

Although beetlelike, cockroaches are actually related to termites and praying mantids. Their fossils date back 350 million to 400 million years. They were so common during this period that this geological time period has become known as the "Age of Cockroaches." Fossils of entire cockroaches are rare; most fossils consist mainly of wings, wing fragments, or other body parts. The ancient impressions of cockroach remains clearly demonstrate that these animals have changed little over the millennia.

So, the next time you see a cockroach, take a moment to ponder this amazing creature on its own terms. It is an evolutionary marvel whose ancestors have remained virtually unchanged since before dinosaurs roamed the Earth. Try not to look at this uninvited guest as an intruder, but as a gentle reminder to step up your house-cleaning regimen. And remember, applying yet another toxin to your immediate environment to kill cockroaches should only be done as a last resort, after you have removed all of the resources that brought them into your home in the first place.

Ants: Movers and Shakers of the Natural World

Safely tucked away from the lethal tendrils of ice, deep within our walls, under our homes, buried in the soil, or hidden beneath tree bark, is arguably Virginia's most voracious predator, the ant. But with the flush of warmth that marks the arrival of spring, these tiny marauders will be out hunting and scavenging in force—negotiating the tangles of garden and woodland growth, as well as the complexities of your kitchen counter, with equal aplomb.

Like us, ants are movers and shakers in the natural world. The relentless quest for food and space of some twelve thousand species around the world has shaped entire habitats, thanks to their activities of dispersing seeds, pruning and clearing vegetation, and culling insects and other small animals. The digging activities and soil aeration services rendered by ants exceed that of earthworms. And many species benefit plants directly by spreading and planting seeds, even driving away leaf-feeding caterpillars and beetles.

Ants are completely social, living in complex societies of hundreds to millions of individuals and populated by overlapping generations that care for the brood, obtain food, enlarge the nest, and defend the colony. These duties are usually divided up among workers of different sizes. Depending on the species, a special caste of soldiers with enlarged heads and mandibles is charged with repelling nest invaders. With the exception of mating males and queens, all ants in the nest are sterile females. Only queens lay viable eggs, and do so by the hundreds or thousands every day of their adult lives for up to several years.

Their success is due to their incredible ability to cooperate and communicate with each other using volatile chemical compounds known as pheromones. Released from various parts of their bodies, ant pheromones entreat other ants of the same colony to regurgitate food, find tasty treats, or enlist their defense of the colony.

All ants can bite, but not all of them sting. Some biters will ratchet up the pain by spraying the wound with acid, causing a sharp, stinging sensation. Those that do sting do so with a modified egg-laying tube. The sting of the aptly named red imported fire ant, *Solenopsis invicta*, truly burns like fire! Accidentally introduced to the southeastern United States from South America, these primarily insect predators will attack both wild and domesticated animals, especially those that cannot escape. Seldom house pests, the mound-building fire ants are serious pests outdoors in gardens, agricultural fields, and farms. Fortunately, Virginia's cold winters have, thus far, kept this species south of the border.

Human dwellings are fertile hunting grounds for ants, de facto buffets that are ripe for the picking for hungry and thirsty ant colonies. Scouts quickly return to their nests with sample booty, laying down a pheromone trail as they go to mark the way back. This invisible trail alerts hundreds or thousands of nest mates and guides them to the goodies. Each ant using the trail reinforces it with its own pheromones to recruit still more ants. Ants often invade homes during hot, dry weather in search of water, but will also move indoors to avoid cold or wet weather.

To secure your home from ants, use silicone caulk to plug and seal holes and cracks in walls, especially around plumbing and windows. Powdered charcoal or cleansers, cayenne pepper, or diatomaceous earth can be used to create impenetrable, irritating barriers to ants as well. A solid line no more than a quarter inch will help to keep ants out, but may have to be reapplied after rains. Placing honey containers and pet food in bowls of soapy water will create impenetrable moats to ants. Wipe up spills immediately and store foods in sealed containers. Dead insects that accumulate on windowsills are also attractive to some house ants and should be removed frequently.

The simplest, most inexpensive, and least toxic material to control ants is soapy water. Simply place a teaspoon of dish soap in a spray bottle full of water and douse your uninvited guests with the solution. The soap acts as a wetting agent, allowing the water to penetrate and clog the breathing pores located on the sides of their bodies. The soapy water also eliminates their scent trails. Glass cleaner also does the trick.

You can launch an effective control program by following household ants back to their nests. Hose the nest with water until the workers come boiling up to the surface with their brood looking for higher ground and spray them with soapy water. Keep garbage, plant debris, firewood, and ivy away from buildings to reduce ant and other crawling insect and spider traffic from entering your home.

The best way to achieve long-term control of ants is to bait them. Commercially available bait stations brimming with incredibly toxic stuff are overkill. Instead, look for brands that use boric acid as the main ingredient. This slow-acting toxin gives ants plenty of time to carry the tainted bait back to the nest and feed it to their sisters, who, with luck, will eventually pass a lethal dose along to your logical and ultimate target, the queen. This method is slow, but sure.

Before arming yourself with soap and boric acid for an all-out battle, keep in mind that, next to spiders, ants are among the most effective natural controls of insects. Flies, caterpillars, and other small crawling insects succumb to their depredations. The predatory activities of ants in gardens may even keep house-gnawing termites at bay. Indoors, ants are known to eat the eggs and larvae of fleas, prey on cockroaches, and might even attack silverfish, clothes moths, and various other closet and pantry pests.

To see some very cool pictures of ants, visit http://myrmecos .net/ants.html.

The Black Widow

I can still remember the first time I saw a black widow more than forty years ago. Her plump, shiny body was suspended upside down with the red hourglass facing up in a messy web situated in a dark corner of our garage. I immediately recoiled from my discovery. I don't recall my parents lecturing me on the potential hazards of a black widow bite; my reaction was more visceral.

Years later, while working as a consultant for a company building giant robotic insects and spiders for the traveling exhibit Backyard Monsters, I had the opportunity to revisit the object of my youthful discomfort. I was charged with selecting several species for use in the exhibit, and knew that we had to include a widow. The designers, photographers, sculptors, and engineers all shared my instinctive apprehension of this animal. We rightly guessed that a detailed robot, fifty-four times life-size and accurate down to every bump and bristle, would grab audiences of all ages across the country.

The notoriety of black widow spiders stems, in part, from their venomous bites. Ounce for ounce, the venom of these spiders is fifteen times more potent than that of a rattlesnake. However, the amount of venom, a neurotoxin, injected into the wound, is relatively small. Symptoms of their bites include local tenderness, severe muscular pain and stiffness, sweating, and vomiting.

Fortunately, black widows are not aggressive spiders. Their bites are easily avoided simply by not putting hands or feet in places where spiders might be hiding. And wearing gloves when working in the basement, garage, or yard will provide ample protection from their small and relatively weak fangs. In the unlikely event of a bite, keep calm, place a bag of ice on the wound, and seek medical treatment immediately. Fatalities from widow bites are very rare, although small children, the elderly, and persons already in poor health can become seriously ill.

Black widows are also known for devouring their mates. Amorous males cautiously approach a female's web and gently give it a tug to let her know that he is a mate and not a meal. He then vibrates his abdomen on the web. If receptive, the female responds in kind. As he approaches her, he begins stroking her legs with his. If she is still receptive, he spins a delicate web around her just before inseminating her. Contrary to popular belief, he has about a fifty-fifty chance of escaping her silken boudoir with his life.

There are three species of black widows in the United States, two of which occur in Virginia. They all belong to the worldwide genus *Latrodectus*, which means "stealing biter." The northern widow, *L. variolus*, is found throughout eastern United States and southern Canada. It has red spots on its back as well as the red hourglass underneath. The southern widow, *L. mactans*, known mainly from the southeastern United States but also occurring as far north as southeastern Canada, lacks any red markings on the back. The western widow, *L. hesperus*, is found in western United States and Canada.

Mature female black widows are known practically to all, thanks to their glossy black or dark brown bodies usually marked underneath with a distinct red hourglass. Adult males are short-lived and are only a third of the size of the female. They are tan or black with white streaks across the top of the abdomen and resemble young females. Their small size and short fangs render males obscure and harmless to humans.

The strong, low, messy webs of the females are spun outdoors in woodpiles, stumps, under rocks, and in abandoned rodent burrows. Indoors, they set up housekeeping in closets, attics, and basements. Their webs are constructed of extremely strong silk, with each strand having ten times the tensile strength of a steel wire of the same diameter. During World War II, black widow silk was harvested and used for the cross hairs in gun sights.

The female deposits from three hundred to five hundred round eggs in a silken sac that looks and feels like parchment paper. The eggs hatch in two to four weeks, but the young spiderlings remain in the sac until the next molt. When ready to venture out on their own, the spiderlings use their saliva to dissolve the silk and escape the egg sac.

Two additional species of *Latrodectus* occur in the United States, neither of which is black. The red widow, *L. bishopi*, is a very handsomely marked species known only from the sand pine scrub habitat of central Florida. The brown widow, *L. geometricus*, is an Old World species that is now found throughout the tropical regions of the world and has turned up here and there in the southern United States from California to Florida.

For more information on black widows, visit http://www.ext .vt.edu/departments/entomology/factsheets/blackwid.html.

For more information on widow bites, see http://www.emedicine .com/EMERG/topic546.htm#.

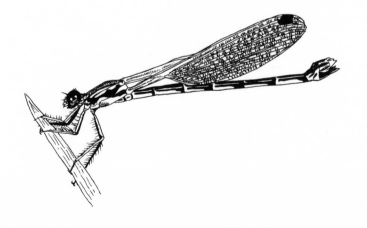

2

On Safari
in Virginia

One of the definite perks of being an entomologist is that the objects of my obsession, insects and their relatives, are everywhere, a fact that leaves some people a bit uneasy. But to me, they represent a never-ending parade that always instills in me a sense of wonder and awe. True, some of these animals live among us in the darkest recesses of our homes, but most species prefer living out of doors. Some have even managed to adapt to the lush growth of exotic plants that populate our yards and gardens. But these artificial environments have little to offer most native insect species. As a result, our homes, gardens, and other "disturbed habitats" tend to be decidedly lackluster in terms of species diversity. Instead, these habitats tend to support relatively monotonous insect and spider fauna that afford few surprises when compared to more natural environments.

If you really want to see and appreciate the greatest number of native insects and spiders, you have to get out of the house, leave your neighborhood, and venture out into wilder places. If you are short on time, city parks can be a great place to start, as long as they are not managed like a garden. Expanses of mowed grass and neatly pruned trees and shrubs can be pleasing to the eye, but they are not particularly productive places for bug- and spider-watching. The rewards will be much greater if you seek out the less tidy sections of these parks. The diversity of insects, spiders, and other animals in parks is directly proportional to the amount of weedy growth, tangled vines, dense thickets, and fallen trees. It is these environs that provide native species with the food, shelter, and nesting places they need in order to survive and thrive. To find such a habitat within the confines of a town or city is to discover a veritable island paradise, an oasis surrounded by a relatively in-hospitable sea of exotic plants, concrete, and asphalt.

Once you get glimpse of Virginia's rich diversity of insect and spider life, chances are you will want to see and learn more. You can easily build up your "BQ," or "bug quotient," by adding different habitats to the mix, day and night. Explore the shores and waters of swamps, ponds, streams, and rivers for species that are dependent on these waters for their development. You can go even farther afield to visit a nearby state or national park, where large tracts of pristine habitats are home to a mind-boggling array of insect and spider species.

On Safari
in Bryan Park

Located at the junction of Interstates 64 and 95, Joseph P. Bryan Park is a remarkable 280 acres of woodlands, gardens, and fields. The park is the home and breeding grounds of countless plants and animals and is particularly rich in insect and spider life. Largely unseen and unappreciated, they are nevertheless an integral part of the park's ecosystem.

Plant-feeding insects, though lamented and condemned by gardeners and foresters alike, provide a natural pruning service that encourages seed germination by both opening up the forest floor to sunlight and fertilizing the soil with their waste. Without the pollination services of bees, flies, and other insects, many of the park's flowering plants would be incapable of producing seeds. And predatory insects and spiders help to keep the plant-feeding insects in check by eating their eggs, larvae, pupae, and adults.

The FBI—fungus, bacteria, and insects—the agents of decomposition, attack the remains of dead plants, animals, fungi, and other organisms and work in concert to break down their tissues and recycle their nutrients for later use by other organisms. But most visitors in the park all too often overlook or are totally unaware of these animals or their critically essential activities. Yet, insects and spiders are surprisingly easy to observe as they go about their daily routines.

With the arrival of spring, insects begin to stir from their winter sleep, crawling out from chambers deep in the soil, beneath tree bark, or secreted in rotten wood. Their emergence is timed perfectly to fuel the waves of hungry, insectivorous birds migrating up from the Caribbean and South America.

The first warm days of late winter and spring are heralded by the sudden appearance of rapidly flying butterflies, such as mourning cloaks and question marks, careening down Jordan's Branch trail.

The mourning cloak's purplish black wings are trimmed in a series of blue spots and a broad yellow border, making the butterfly quite conspicuous when it lands on a bit of bare ground to warm itself in the low sun. The bright orange question mark bursts into view, only to quickly conceal itself among dead leaves. It achieves this feat by simply by closing its wings, whose undersides reveal somber patterns resembling dead leaves.

Where did these butterflies suddenly come from? By carefully tucking themselves into the crevices of tree bark or some other protected place the previous fall, they manage to escape the freezing temperatures of winter. They remain primed and ready to take flight at the slightest hint of warmer temperatures.

Bark stink bugs are difficult to see at first; their rough gray bodies are perfectly camouflaged against the bark of oaks and other trees. You have probably already seen these stinkers in the fall and winter when they've hitched a ride into your home on pieces of firewood. Bark stink bugs use their strawlike piercing-sucking mouthparts primarily to imbibe vital fluids from leaves, but they will occasionally tap into a juicy caterpillar or two to draw their blood.

Packets of eastern tent caterpillar eggs deposited on the twigs of trees by plump, tawny moths last summer are timed to hatch with the first flush of spring leaf growth. Gregarious by nature, the larvae gather in the crotch of a branch to spin a communal tent of silk produced by specialized salivary glands. The beautiful sky blue patches of scales that adorn the flanks of the mature caterpillars belie their destructive nature; their ravenous hordes can strip branches of their leaves in relatively short order.

Even dead logs are teeming with life, especially charter members of the FBI. Conspicuous, inch-long shiny black insects called bess, or patent-leather, beetles use their powerful jaws to gnaw tunnels through moist, rotten logs, eventually reducing them to piles of sawdust. They live in loosely formed colonies of larvae and adults. The digestion of wood by these beetles and other wood-feeding insects is frequently aided by the presence of microorganisms called flagellates living inside their gut. Without these intestinal partners, most wood-feeding insects would soon starve, unable to digest the primary component of wood: cellulose. Like other wood-feeding insects, bess beetles are not born with flagellates but must acquire them as larvae by eating regurgitated food or waste already spiked with these beneficial cellulose busters.

Centipedes, distant relatives of insects and spiders, sometimes brood their eggs in chambers carefully dug beneath logs and stones. They wrap their bodies like a protective shield around the eggs, resembling an oddly segmented bowl filled with yellowish pearls. Female centipedes continually turn and stroke the eggs with their antennae and mouthparts to wash them with saliva laced with a fungicide that protects the eggs from lethal infections of mold.

At the height of summer, the warm, moist air pulsates with the mating calls of male cicadas and the buzzings other flying insects. The park's meadow is in full bloom, supporting a plethora of insect and spider life. Formerly a dump for tree stumps, the meadow's soils are rich in organic materials, supporting a mixture of exotic and native flowering plants that grow waist-high or taller.

Later in the season, hidden among the flowers, is a remarkable sit-and-wait predator known as the ambush bug. Masters of camouflage, ambush bugs conceal themselves among flowers, where they remain motionless until they suddenly attack with lightning speed, capturing insects in the vicelike grip of their almost mantidlike forelegs. They frequently pounce on insects much larger than themselves, such as bees, beetles, butterflies, and flies. Using their long, tubelike mouthparts as both syringe and straw, ambush bugs inject liquefying chemicals into their victims and drain their bodies of fluid. Ambush bugs are often found in pairs with the small male riding on the back of a much larger female.

Another cryptically colored predator is the crab spider, whose white, pink, or yellow body makes it nearly invisible among the flowers. Curious onlookers who have stopped to admire a fly or bee "resting" on a flower often discover that these hapless creatures have fallen victim to one of these spiders. Closer inspection reveals that the insects are dead and firmly in the jaws of the spider.

Scattered along the margins of the soccer fields are the telltale signs of African dung beetles. First introduced into the Southeast more than thirty years ago, these small scarabs have spread throughout much of the southern half of the United States. Working singly or in pairs, they discreetly assist careless dog owners with the task of cleaning up after their pets, burying feces bit by bit, leaving in their wakes only small piles of freshly turned earth. Burrows are dug immediately below the offensive piles and stocked with carefully prepared balls of the stuff. Newly hatched grubs immediately begin feeding on the balls. As their food supply is exhausted, the grubs will transform into pupae. The next generation of these sanitation engineers will emerge within a few weeks or the following spring.

Spring and summer rains regularly swell the banks of Jordan's Branch, washing down a seemingly endless supply of tires, lawn chairs, plastic soda bottles, and other trash. As the floodwaters recede, the plants along the banks are festooned with bits of gaily colored plastic bags, resembling the flags along a parade route. In spite of its tainted waters, Jordan's Branch still manages to support a few hardy aquatic species. Ebony jewelwings—damselflies with shimmering metallic green bodies and dark iridescent wings— haunt the shadows along the stream and its adjacent woods. The aquatic larvae earn their living by capturing mosquito larvae and other small creatures with the aid of a prehensile lower lip.

As fall approaches, the thick tangles of vines and weedy plants line Bryan Park's roads and fill the meadow. Here among the low tangles of growth are female black and yellow garden spiders hanging head down in their intricate orb webs of radiating spokes joined by concentric circles. These sticky aerial traps are engineered to absorb the impact of flying insects, slowing them down enough so that they become tangled and mired in the sticky glue of the web. The spiders wrap their prey with sheets of silk like a mummy, simultaneously killing and liquefying the victim's internal organs with a single, venomous bite. The black and yellow garden spiders are hardly a threat; their delicate mouthparts are designed for puncturing the bodies of insects and not the tough hide of humans.

In late summer and fall, the female pigeon horntail selects the trunks of living hardwoods to lay her eggs. This stingless wasp uses her short, stout egg-laying tube to bore tunnels up to one-half inch deep in the wood. As she injects her eggs into the hole, she also inoculates the tunnel with a special fungus that rots the surrounding wood. As the wasp larvae grow, they bore through the wood as they consume the fungus. Dead females are sometimes found clinging to tree trunks by their egg-laying tubes like a macabre black and orange ornament.

As the autumn nights grow cooler, Bryan Park's insects and spiders seem to take on a new sense of urgency. Depending upon the species, they will spend the winter as eggs, larvae, pupae, or adults. Tucked safely out of harm's way, they will soon offer little outward evidence of their presence at all. But even in the dead of winter, the dried, shriveled branches are alive with the egg cases of praying mantids, the chrysalids of butterflies, and various stages of other insects. Hollow stems and other tiny sheltered spaces offer refuge from the cold to future generations of insects and spiders of all stripes, affording them places to hunker down and wait out the winter.

Soon the approach of another spring will trigger yet another flurry of activity, stirring to action those tiny creatures lucky enough to have escaped predators, parasites, killing frosts, as well as the equally lethal blades of the city's mowers.

To find out more about Bryan Park, visit http://www.friendsof bryanpark.org.

Exploring the Grassroot Jungles of Three Lakes Park

One of the jewels of Henrico County's Division of Recreation and Parks, Three Lakes Park began as a gravel quarry in the 1950s. Three depressions were dug to collect sand and gravel for the construction of Interstate 95. They gradually filled with water from underground springs to form—you guessed it—three lakes.

The park features the impressive 3,000-square-foot Three Lakes Nature Center built by the county in 1992 and expanded in 1999. The center is filled with hands-on activities and special exhibits focusing on native plants and animals of Virginia. It also houses a large collection of local reptiles and amphibians. A giant aquarium teeming with native fish can be viewed from an outside deck or inside the center through underwater windows. Members of the Richmond Herp and Bug Society regularly get together at the nature center. This informal group of naturalists is dedicated to the study of nature, especially reptiles, amphibians, insects, spiders, and other arthropods. Evening spring and summer slide programs are often followed by nocturnal ramblings on the hiking trails.

Although known for its picnic areas, playgrounds, and fishing, the heart of the park lies in its natural treasures. Just over a hundred acres, the park's diverse habitats provide food and shelter for a variety of animals, especially insects and their relatives.

One night, after a Herp and Bug meeting, we came across a seldom-seen mole cricket. Named for their thickly set and clawed front legs, mole crickets are subterranean animals that spend most of their lives tunneling through the soil in search of roots to eat. The male constructs a shallow, Y-shaped tunnel that acts as two megaphones. He then stations himself in the tunnel in a slightly enlarged space that works as a resonating chamber and begins to call. The acoustics of the tunnel compress and amplify his amorous chirps so that they are forced high above the tunnel entrance to catch the attention of high-flying females.

Spring and summer flowers dotting the grounds draw pollen- and nectar-feeding insects of all kinds. Bumblebee moths, distant cousins to the three-inch, sausagelike hornworms that nibble the foliage of our tomatoes, eggplants, and peppers, dart from flower to flower. Unlike bumblebees, these day-active moths hover over each blossom like a hummingbird, unfurling their long tongues like party favors to drink the nectar produced by deep-throated blooms. Unlike most moths and butterflies, they have large translucent patches on their otherwise scaly wings, enhancing their beelike appearance.

Scattered about in loose, dry, sandy soils are distinctive conical pits that serve as the lairs of young antlions, known to many as doodlebugs. Each doodlebug moves its wedge-shaped body backward in ever-tightening circles, using its flat head as a shovel to excavate the pit. Once completed, the antlion lies in wait at the bottom just beneath the sand.

When an ant or other small, hapless creatures tumbles in, the antlion clamps down on its victim using its ice tong–like mandibles with lightning speed. The mandibles are hollow and are first used as syringes to inject digestive enzymes into the body of the prey, and later as straws to suck out the liquefied internal organs.

Three Lakes is a haven for summer dragonfly-watching. Armed with nothing more than a pair of close-focusing binoculars and a field guide, even the casual observer can easily identify several species in a day, including blue dashers, common whitetails, and eastern pond meadowhawks.

The branches of the red cedars surrounding the picnic areas are the stage for one of nature's most amazing partnerships. Here plump, grayish aphids tap their long, strawlike mouthparts into the cedar's supple branches to drink sap. They produce waste as honeydew, a clear sticky fluid rich in carbohydrates. Ants are particularly fond of honeydew and will milk and tend the aphids as if they were cattle. In return, the ants drive off ladybugs, parasitic wasps, and other aphid enemies in defense of their six-legged kegs of honeydew.

Reddish orange and black large milkweed bugs typically inhabit the foliage, stems, and seedpods of milkweeds here and there in the park. Although the toxic and bitter plant tissues of the milkweed deter most animals, milkweed bugs feed on the seeds without ill effect and incorporate the plant's chemical defense system as their own. The bugs advertise the fact that they too taste bad by sporting bright, contrasting colors.

This tiny parcel of reclaimed land is a gentle reminder of Virginia's all too fragmented and fragile natural heritage. In a time of unprecedented development and habitat modification, Three Lakes Park still manages to serve as an oasis to many forms of wildlife, both with and without backbones. Three Lakes Nature Center and Aquarium is located north of Richmond at 400 Sausulita Drive, Richmond, Virginia 23227. Admission is free. For more information and seasonal hours of operation call (804) 261-8230.

Dragonfly- and damselfly-watchers should visit the Odonata-Dragonfly Diversity Web site at http://www.ups.edu/x5666.xml.

Postscript. On August 30, 2004, Tropical Storm Gaston dumped up to a foot and a half of rain on Richmond in a twenty-four-hour period. Normally quiet creeks and sleepy streams turned into raging torrents, sending destructive walls of water and mud in all directions, including that of the Three Lakes Nature Center. The rising waters of the lake immediately adjacent to the nature center breached its banks, sending two feet of water into the building. Fish were washed right out of the aquarium. And anything within two feet above the floor, such as animals, books, and supplies, was either drowned or destroyed. Without a regular place to meet, attendance at the Richmond Herp and Bug Society meetings plummeted; the group held its last meeting in September 2005. A new organization, the Virginia Society of Naturalists, arose in its place and meets the third Tuesday of each month (except during summer) at the Science Museum of Virginia in Richmond. The Three Lakes Nature Center reopened in 2007.

Tiny Game Hunting
along the James River

I have anticipated the arrival of spring and summer since the last warm days of October. Having spent most of my life in the drier environs of southern California, I find Virginia's vernal explosion of flowers, lush vegetation, and teeming insect life new and incredibly exciting. The hum of insect activity in the warm spring air fills me with a new sense of purpose and drives me outdoors to explore, see, and learn.

One of my favorite haunts for bug-watching lies smack dab in the middle of Richmond. The James River Park snakes through the heart of the city like a riverine jewel, a riparian oasis offering countless opportunities to reconnect with a slice of wild Virginia. At least once a week I set out for the park's Northbank, Belle Isle, Reedy Creek, Wetlands, or Pony Pasture to watch the seasons come and go. During the warmer months, I wander along their sun-dappled paths and roads in search of some of Virginia's most overlooked and certainly least appreciated inhabitants: insects and spiders.

Isolated, sunny patches of earth scattered about the hardwood forest floor are the favorite haunts of the six-spotted tiger beetle, one of the flashiest predators around. Dressed in brilliant green armor punctuated by three small enameled white spots on each wing cover, these bug-eyed animals measure no more than ½ inch in length. They hunt for any small insect prey, seizing them between their scythelike mandibles.

The season's first generation of tiger and zebra swallowtails appears in April, freshly emerged from the winterlong confinement of their pupae. As they take to the air, their wings seem to alternate between slow, measured strokes and fits of rapid-fire beats. Dark-winged and thick-bodied skippers power through the woods, emerging in the sunlight only to disappear again into the shadows. Tiny blue butterflies and angular-winged question marks soak up the sun along the park's open spaces, occasionally stopping at mud puddles to imbibe salts and water.

Vines of poison ivy cling to the trunks of trees, forced to climb upward in search of light. Like all plants, this temperate cousin to the cashew and mango is not immune to the ravages of herbivorous insects. The larvae of the poison ivy sawfly, a crimson and black stingless wasp, resemble caterpillars and focus their ravenous appetites on the toxic leaves of both poison ivy and poison sumac.

In the heat and humidity of summer, long-faced and amber-colored scorpionflies flit about the low herbaceous growth, borne on four delicate and distinctly banded wings. These insects are so named because of the stingerlike reproductive organ located on the tip of the male's abdomen. In spite of this adornment, scorpionflies cannot sting and are incapable of inflicting any harm on humans.

Courting males have several options for wooing females. They can either capture a small insect to offer as a nuptial meal or steal one from another male. Or they can regurgitate a gummy, yet nutritious globule that serves the same purpose as the nuptial offering. As a last resort, they can simply grasp the wings of the female with a special device on their abdomens called the notal organ and force their attentions on otherwise reluctant females.

Mayflies and stoneflies also sun themselves on the leaves. They have spent most of their lives as larvae feeding in the muck covering the river bottom. Rocks, logs, and objects rising out of the river are frequently littered with the ghostlike husks of their youthful bodies, their backs burst open to allow the escape of emerging adults.

An important part of the diet for many fish living in the James, these insects serve as models for countless flies and lures used by anglers trying to get a bite. A good fly fisherman must also be a good aquatic entomologist to know which aquatic insects have just emerged. Armed with this knowledge, the observant angler can then select the appropriate fly that mimics what the fish are eating.

The James River Park is a not only a refuge for both insects and naturalists; it also offers other nearby residents a rejuvenating respite from the pressures of city life. To me, the reappearance of these and other familiar insects after a long, cold winter is akin to seeing old friends. The quiet comfort experienced by observing this annual renewal and rebirth is the perfect antidote to our all-too-hectic lives.

To find out more about the James River Park, see http://www .ci.richmond.va.us/departments/parks/james.aspx.

To become a Friend of the James River, visit http://www.james riverpark.org/.

Nighttime Bug-Watching at Pocahontas State Park

It's late afternoon. The air is hot and thick, draped like a hazy, wet blanket over the landscape. The dull orange sun hangs heavy over the tops of trees lining the lake and soon drops out of sight. Whirligig beetles drift lazily in the placid water, barely leaving a ripple in their wake. Dragonflies dart back and forth, gobbling up their final meals of midges and other tiny flying insects for the day.

As dusk approaches, the throbbing wail of cicadas loses its urgency and eventually stops, as do the relentless attacks of bloodsucking deer flies. The barn swallows that had ruled the skies for most of the afternoon are now settled in for the night, giving way to their mammalian counterparts, bats. Several of these amazing insect predators skim the lake's surface right in front of me to drink from the still water.

I am in the vicinity of Group Camp 7 in the southernmost reaches of Pocahontas State Park. Normally accessible only on foot or by horseback, this sylvan oasis within the park definitely has a feel of remoteness seldom experienced so close to a major metropolitan area.

With more than 7,600 acres, Pocahontas is the largest state park in Virginia. Located just twenty miles southwest of downtown Richmond, the park is probably best known for its swimming pool, camping and conference facilities, outdoor performances, and music festivals. But it is also a favorite haunt among local naturalists, especially birders. I visit the park regularly to observe and photograph Virginia insect life during the spring and summer.

As the day shift winds down, the creatures of the night slowly begin to stir, gearing up to take their place on the evening stage. With the arrival of twilight, there seems to be a moment or two when all insect life seems to pause ever so briefly, and then the night shift takes over.

The twinkling lights of amorous lightningbugs, or fireflies, begin to appear about the low growth sprinkled over the woodland floor. Neither bugs nor flies, these soft-bodied insects are actually beetles. Males engage in a slow, looping flight with repeated dips to create a J-pattern with their lights. At the bottom of the descent, their abdomen glows bright yellowish green, becoming dimmer before shutting off completely at the top of their ascent. Their oversized compound eyes are trained on the not-so-distant darkness, hoping to see the light of a stationary female responding with her own perfectly timed and pulsating response perched low among the weedy growth.

Later in the evening another species appears, flying high and fast in the canopy, releasing its light in rapid bursts of three. Fireflies have developed this system of luminous Morse code to locate mates of their own kind among the tangled growth and to avoid fruitless encounters with the wrong species.

Chunky June beetles begin to rustle among the leaf litter and slowly rise into the air from their daytime hiding places with a buzz. They plow through the night as if they were trucks in low gear, slowly gaining speed as they begin their nightly search for mates and fresh leaves to eat.

With a headlamp strapped to my sweaty head, I venture forth like a bright-eyed Cyclops in search of more of the commonwealth's nocturnal insect and spider fauna. The forest floor seems to glitter with tiny stars, which turn out to be the tiny, unblinking eyes of wolf spiders reflecting the beam of my light. They, too, are searching for insects.

As my headlamp cuts through the rapidly darkening night, moths, beetles, and other airborne insects fly in and out of the sharp beam. Some crash into my face as they frantically flap about to reach the light's source.

For years, entomologists have taken advantage of the fact that many insects are attracted to lights at night. Using the ultraviolet component of distant light to orient themselves, many insects are uncontrollably drawn to nearby artificial lights, such as flickering campfires, hissing gas lanterns, brightly lit storefronts, and street-lights—not the sad, dull yellowish lights that inhabit city streets, but the bright, inviting glow of mercury vapor lights that illumi-nate the lesser-populated areas.

Lights strong in the ultraviolet spectrum are especially attrac-tive to nocturnal insects. I use several BL black lights specifically for attracting night-flying insects. Set in front of and above white sheets for reflectivity and contrast, and powered with a 12-volt gel cell battery, the lights emanate an eerie purple glow that works like a bug zapper, but without the zap.

Warm, humid, moonless, or overcast skies seem to be the best nights to "black-light" for insects since there is less ultraviolet light to compete with my setup. The greatest insect activity at lights is right after dark, between 9:30 and 11:00 PM, although some of the larger beetles and moths are usually fashionably late and seldom make an appearance before midnight.

Nocturnal insects can easily maintain a steady flight path in relation to distant sources of light. However, they must fly in ever-tighter spirals in order to maintain their orientation to a nearby light source. Eventually they alight on the sheet or nearby vegeta-tion. If left undisturbed, most would remain within sight of the light until dawn, when the rising sun would drive them to seek shelter from the heat and hungry birds.

As night falls, insects swirl about my black light like small com-ets. My sheet was soon covered in a dizzying array of insects rang-ing from tiny gnats just millimeters long, to relatively giant mayflies and June beetles. Dozens of plump, fuzzy moths of all colors settled on the sheet like fighter planes on the deck of an aircraft carrier. Shiny, smooth, and streamlined aquatic beetles emerged from the nearby lake and clambered awkwardly beneath the light, like proverbial fish out of water. About two hundred different species of insects in all made an appearance at the light. The preparation and identification of this relatively small showing would require the full-time efforts of an entomologist for at least a year.

Occasionally a bat hurtled through the cloud of insects, gobbling them up as if it were bellying up to an airborne buffet. Using a series of high-pitched clicks like radar to locate airborne insects, the bats dart and bank sharply through the night air in pursuit of hapless insects.

But not all insects are defenseless against bats. Some moths and mantids have special "ears" capable of picking up the signals bats use for their echolocation system. Upon hearing the call of a nearby bat, these insects will take sudden evasive action by pulling in their wings and dropping to the ground or making a spiral power dive to safety.

After 11:00 PM, the waves of incoming insects began to slow to a mere trickle. I packed up just after midnight, but the choruses of frogs, katydids, and crickets continued to rise and fall. Although I am sure that these incredible performances sound like a raucous cacophony to many, I found the chirps, clicks, buzzes, twangs, and bellows to be joyous noise, the perfect sound track for an evening out with the night shift.

For directions or more information on interpretive programs and events at Pocahontas State Park, call (804) 796-4255, or visit http://www.dcr.virginia.gov/state-parks/poc.shtml.

Wet and Wild

During the winter, hundreds of different kinds of aquatic insects are hidden beneath the icy surfaces of Virginia's ponds and along the shores of her slow-moving rivers and sluggish streams. Buried in the mud or tucked away among the waterlogged bits of leaves and wood, these dormant denizens of the deep are in a state of suspended animation as they wait for the first hints of spring.

With the arrival of the first warm days of the season, rafts of shiny, torpedo-shaped beetles leave their winter hideaways and gather on the water's surface. Without warning, these seemingly docile aggregations of whirligigs suddenly explode in frenetic activity, with each beetle gyrating wildly like ricocheting bullets on the water surface. But soon, this chaotic mass of beetles coalesces once again into a placid flotilla.

Whirligigs take full advantage of the water's surface tension, which creates a smooth, slippery membrane that serves as both a transportation system and a buffet counter. Their streamlined bodies are propelled on the surface by four flat, paddlelike legs and steered by the remarkably flexible rudderlike tip of their abdomen. The forelegs of these sleek, black predators are designed for grasping hapless insect prey trapped on the water surface.

Like whirligigs, leggy water striders are supremely adapted for living on the surface of ponds, lakes, and other slow-moving rivers. Virtually unsinkable, they use their middle legs to propel themselves across the water, while steering with their hind legs. The short forelegs are used for grabbing insect prey and sending or receiving messages in the form of waves on the surface of the water; they use surface waves to attract mates and locate prey.

Beneath the surface of quiet pools, backswimmers use their flat, oarlike hind legs to propel themselves upside down through the water. Their fore- and middle legs are used to capture insect prey and cling to submerged objects while they rest. Hanging upside down at an angle, backswimmers acquire their air supply by breaking the surface film with the bristly tips of their abdomens to draw an air bubble over their backs.

Water scorpions lurk along the edges of ponds fringed by emergent vegetation. Perfectly camouflaged among submerged plants, their long and slender bodies resemble a cross between a walking stick and a mantid. Poor swimmers, water scorpions must stay close to the water's edge and breathe through a snorkel-like respiratory tube extending from the tip of their abdomen to the surface of the water. With mantidlike forelegs at the ready, they lie in wait for mosquito larvae, water fleas, and small aquatic organisms.

A more robust cousin of the water scorpion, giant water bugs live up to their name, measuring in at a whopping three inches in length. Also known as electric light bugs, these large and showy insects sometimes fly to lights as they search for new ponds at night. To breathe underwater, a giant water bug traps an air bubble between its wings by exposing the tip of its abdomen above water.

The presence or absence of these and other aquatic insects, especially those living in cold-water streams, is used as a measure of environmental health. Subtle changes in water quality, such as increases in temperature or chemical pollutants, trigger responses in insects finely tuned to specific stream conditions. To survive these changing conditions, aquatic insects must either adapt or emigrate, or they will soon perish. Changes in their populations as a result of these and other environmental perturbations are observed long before similar changes occur in most vertebrate and plant populations, giving scientists an important early warning system for monitoring water quality.

The Virginia BioBlitz: A Snapshot of Biodiversity

The inaugural Virginia BioBlitz, held at Pocahontas State Park in May 2002, brought together nearly one hundred biologists, students, amateurs, and volunteers to participate in an intensive twenty-four-hour survey of plants and animals. The event not only raised the public's awareness of Virginia's incredible biological diversity, it also helped to build relationships among the commonwealth's professional and amateur biologists. The synergy created through new contacts and shared insights will benefit the study of Virginia's biodiversity for years to come.

Organizing the BioBlitz was a team effort requiring the cooperation of several state agencies, museums, and universities. Experts were recruited from various fields of biology to act as team leaders. The allure for many participants, who came from all over Virginia and as far away as Illinois, was simply the challenge of finding and identifying as many species as possible within their area of specialty.

The activities of seventeen inventory teams covering five kingdoms of organisms were coordinated and supported by a crack team of Department of Conservation and Recreation personnel, environmental educators, and data collectors.

The heart of the BioBlitz was a dining hall that served as both laboratory and dormitory. Half of the hall was a maze of tables laden with the tools of the trade for field biologists: microscopes, field guides, scientific papers, collecting equipment, and specimens. The other half of the building was strewn with sleeping bags, mattresses, pillows, and other sleeping paraphernalia.

The data-collecting station consisted of two laptop computers, one for plants and one for animals. Whether an organism was identified as the red maple, *Acer rubrum,* or simply tagged as beetle no. 1201, volunteers carefully entered the data for each species into a database maintained by the staff of Virginia Division of Natural Heritage.

At noon on Saturday all but one team fanned out into the park to begin their surveys. The bat team would not take to the field until after dark; once they were on the ground, their activities would carry on through the night, ending just before sunrise. The teams covering flowering plants and vertebrates observed most of their organisms in the field, checked the names off, and submitted their final lists to the data compilers.

Armed with a tool belt full of bottles, soil-digging and bark-prying implements, and a net, I set off in search of as many beetles as I could find. To boost my numbers, I engaged in the tried-and-true method of setting out numerous traps baited with rotting shrimp, fish, and bits of dung. The allure of stench and death alone added approximately twenty species to the list.

The nonvascular plant and invertebrate teams collected short series of voucher specimens for preparation and identification in the makeshift lab back at the base camp. Although many of the insects were readily identified as distinct species by their form alone, I knew it would take many months of hard work before most of them were correctly assigned a scientific name. Five years later, I am still laboring to identify all of the nearly three hundred species of beetles collected on that day in May.

Our knowledge of the distribution, occurrence, and patterns of life here in the commonwealth is fragmentary at best. The ebb and flow of plant and animal life at Pocahontas State Park and elsewhere changes dramatically with time of day, temperature, humidity, and season. A complete inventory in just one day is simply impossible. Still, the list of species generated by the 2002 Virginia BioBlitz provides a potentially useful resource for the land-use managers of the state park system.

Just hours before the official end of the BioBlitz at noon on Sunday, everyone was talking about how much fun they were having. And there was speculation as to when and where the next Virginia BioBlitz would be held. My only regret was that there wasn't more time. Not just to find more species, but rather to bask in the light of so many knowledgeable and enthusiastic biologists and naturalists. Oh, I almost forgot! We logged in 1,377 species.

To find out more about the most recent Virginia BioBlitz, log on to http://fwie.fw.vt.edu/vnhs/bioblitz.htm.

3

Marvels of

Metamorphosis

Over the years, my path has crossed with those whose earliest recollections of nature often involve an intense experience with a butterfly or moth. Some have offered up vivid memories of running through a field or meadow with a homemade butterfly net made out of a broom handle and a coat hanger in hot pursuit of a monarch, tiger swallowtail, or some other large, colorful butterfly. Others recount tales of giant, butterflylike moths drawn to a porch light on a spring or summer night, often remaining on a wall or screen until the next morning. For many, their first up-close-and-personal experience with one of these animals was in the classroom. Students of all ages are treated to the marvel of metamorphosis, thanks to teachers who have procured silk moth or painted lady eggs through a mail-order house on the Internet. Whether intertwined with the thrill of the chase or discovery, these memories last a lifetime. And for many, these experiences have ignited careers as scientists and teachers, or fueled the interest in nature of students and naturalists.

There is also the satisfaction of reading about the habits of butterflies and moths and then going out and collecting their eggs and caterpillars to rear in captivity. For these industrious students of nature, watching their young charges eat, grow, develop, and ultimately transform successfully into a wholly different organism is its own reward. And by diligently recording their observations, these folks can make new and valuable contributions to the scientific study of butterflies and moths.

As for me, these wonderful animals have, in all their stages of life, afforded me with the thrill of the hunt and the discovery of something new. There is something very satisfying and rejuvenating about walking down a wooded trail, or along the edge of an open field laden with flowers in the hopes of finding butterflies, or their eggs, caterpillars, and pupae. And nothing makes me giddier than the anticipation of a good night's black lighting that promises to lure in numerous species of moths and other insects with its eerie purplish glow bouncing off a white sheet or wall. Just these two endeavors alone have provided me with thousands of opportunities around the world to learn something new and have provided plenty of grist for my insect photograph mill. Each and every one of these experiences has reminded me that there is still much to see and learn of these marvelous insects.

Caterpillars: The Long, Dark Underbelly of Butterflies and Moths

Butterflies never suffer the stigma of being pests, or even insects. However, this sympathetic attitude rarely extends to their much more numerous cousins, the moths. Usually dismissed as drab creatures of the dark, these animals are at best out of sight and out of mind, or at worst a clear reminder that we are not always in control of what is lurking in our closets and pantries.

But butterflies and moths all have one thing in common: they spend their formative weeks and months—most of their lives, actually—as caterpillars. And like their adult progenitors, they, too, come in a range of patterns, shapes, and sizes. The name "caterpillar" is derived from the two Latin words meaning "hairy cat." Although many caterpillars are "naked," others are densely hairy or spiny. Some species vary tremendously in color, changing their hue as they grow and mature.

In spite of their overall diversity, caterpillars all have soft, cylindrical bodies with a hard, round head equipped with powerful jaws. They also have up to six pairs of tiny eyes. Each eye is equipped with only a single lens and is capable of little more than differentiating between light and dark. The thorax bears six clawlike legs. The long trunklike abdomen has up to five pairs of fleshy false legs called prolegs. The bottom of each proleg's "foot" is packed with an assortment of hooks, or crochets, that help the caterpillar get a grip on its world.

Watching a caterpillar inch its way up a branch or across a leaf is a real treat. To move, it must first contract muscles at the rear of its body. This action forces blood toward the front of the body and expands it forward. The six thoracic legs anchor the caterpillar at the forward position, and the forward muscles contract to bring up the rear. As the muscle of each proleg relaxes, the blood pressure decreases, causing the crochets to swing down and out to hook into the leaf or stem. When the muscles contract, the proleg is lifted up, simultaneously swinging the crochets up and in, withdrawing them from the leaf. Thus, the rippling, wavelike motion of a caterpillar on the go is the result of muscle tension and controlled fluctuation of blood pressure. This hydrostatic system also keeps the caterpillar's soft exoskeleton turgid without the aid of a stiff supporting internal structure.

The sole job of caterpillars is to eat and grow. Most of them take several weeks to mature, but some species must first hibernate through the winter before resuming growth the following spring. Fresh vegetation fuels the vast majority of caterpillars, but others scavenge bits of dead plants and fungi. Some attack seeds and rotting fruit. These species, such as Indian meal moths, have adapted to the environs of our pantries and other food stores where there is an abundance of stored grains, nuts, and dried fruits. A few species prefer animal tissues and prey on aphids and other caterpillars, or graze on feathers and fur lining the nests of birds and mammals. The infamous clothes moth that invades our closets falls into this last category.

Plump, juicy, and out there for all to see, many caterpillars are fair game for a wide variety of animals. But they are hardly defenseless and have developed numerous strategies to avoid or deter even the hungriest predator. Some are camouflaged to match their leafy backgrounds. Others are cryptically marked and shaped to resemble twigs. Still other species are brightly colored or distinctly patterned to warn potential predators that they are brimming with noxious chemicals. The black, yellow, and white bands of monarch caterpillars serve to warn that their exoskeleton is awash in toxic and distasteful compounds sequestered from their food plant, milkweeds. The mature caterpillars of our official state insect, the eastern tiger swallowtail, are slightly humpbacked with distinct eyespots, giving them a decidedly intimidating and serpentine look.

Many caterpillars are bristling with itching hairs that discourage birds from gulping them down or keep tiny parasitic wasps from landing and laying eggs inside their bodies. Others are defended by an impressive array of stinging spines, each capable of delivering small amounts of venom that will raise painful welts on vertebrate predators, as well as unsuspecting gardeners. The familiar hornworm sports a single spine that juts out from its backside. In spite of their fearsome appearance, hornworms are incapable of inflicting any physical harm.

Other caterpillars hide in silken bivouacs spun from specialized salivary glands in their lower lip. In spring, eastern tent caterpillars spin their protective tents over the crotches of trees and shrubs. They venture out during the day to feed on nearby leaves, but at night or during inclement weather, they remain inside their shelters. Later in the season, fall webworms completely envelop leaves with silken enclosures and remain inside to feed for much of their lives.

Some caterpillars are considered pests. They ravage our gardens and neglected beehives, while others chew their way through woolen sweaters or contaminate stored foods with their webbing and waste. But a few caterpillars are considered beneficial and have found their way into commerce. Probably best known is the silkworm, the world's only completely domesticated insect. They are meticulously fed and pampered so their silk can be harvested from their cocoons. Wax worms are raised and sold as pet food, while other caterpillars are dried or canned and sold as human food in Mexico and southern Africa. Mexican jumping beans, sold as a novelty in this country, get their "jump" from the snapping body contortions of a small moth caterpillar that feeds inside the seed. And butterfly farms raise millions of caterpillars annually and ship them as pupae to butterfly houses throughout North America, Europe, and Southeast Asia.

So the next time you see a caterpillar out and about, give it a break. Better yet, take a larva to lunch by planting native flowers and shrubs in your garden and along roadsides that will sustain its entire life cycle and not just the final, flitting, and flashy stages.

America's First Insect:
The Eastern Tiger Swallowtail

While driving west on I-64 just after a protracted vernal deluge, I saw hundreds of large yellow-and-black butterflies. Most flitted without a care across the road, while others tumbled through the air, swept up in the swirling wake of vehicular traffic racing along at a breakneck speed. For the past several months, these and other eastern tiger swallowtails had clung to life inside their silk-girdled chrysalids. The sudden spring explosion of these butterflies was in direct response to increased sunlight and sustained warmer temperatures.

Next to the monarch, tiger swallowtails are perhaps the best-known butterfly in eastern North America. The black-and-yellow males are typically tiger-striped, but the females come in two color forms. The first resembles the male, but the second is much darker, almost black with a hint of even darker stripes. This darker form is thought to mimic the pipevine swallowtail, a butterfly notorious for its bitter taste.

Males search lush deciduous forests, moist river bottoms, parks, and gardens for mates. During their wild and winged courtship, both sexes emit powerful chemical stimulants, or pheromones. Eggs are laid singly on a variety of plants, including the leaves of apple, wild cherry, magnolia, basswood, tulip tree, birch, ash, cottonwood, and willow. Adults seek nectar on a wide variety of flowers and are frequent visitors to butterfly gardens.

At first the young caterpillars resemble unattractive bird droppings, no doubt as a means of defense. Later they turn green with yellow and blue eyespots on their backs. Before forming a chrysalis, the mature caterpillar spins a silken belt from the specialized salivary glands in its lower lip and lashes itself to a branch. Two generations of tiger swallowtails are produced annually, and adults are found in Virginia from early spring well into October.

These beautiful animals were among the first insects described from North America. In 1587, John Watts, commander of Sir Walter Raleigh's third expedition to Virginia, painted the butterfly. Later, this painting became the basis for a woodcut that appeared in Thomas Mouffet's posthumous magnum opus, *Insectum sive minimorum animalium theatrum,* published in 1634. It was Mouffet's daughter that inspired the classic nursery rhyme "Little Miss Muffet." Later, specimens of tiger swallowtails collected in Virginia made their way to the famous Swedish scientist Carolus Linnaeus (or Carl von Linné, as he is also known), who officially dubbed the butterfly with its Latin moniker, *Papilio glaucus,* in 1758.

In 1976, both the Carolina mantis and the eastern tiger swallowtail were up for consideration to become Virginia's official insect, but the Senate and House each backed different bugs and were deadlocked. The issue languished until 1991, when the Virginia legislature rallied to declare the eastern tiger swallowtail as the official insect. As a result, the butterfly has now taken its place on license plates among the northern cardinal and dogwood as a certified symbol of the commonwealth.

The eastern tiger swallowtail is also recognized as the official state insect for Alabama, Delaware, and South Carolina. Georgia recognizes the tiger swallowtail as its official state butterfly, while the honeybee is the official insect.

Some Caterpillars Lead "In Tents" Lives

One of the surest signs of spring is the appearance of the silken bivouacs of the eastern tent caterpillar, *Malacosoma americanum.* Their protective retreats are conspicuously anchored in the crotches of trees and shrubs, especially on cherry, apple, pecan, pear, plum, and other members of the rose family. They also infest many other shade trees and broadleaf plants.

Inside the tents dwell dozens of writhing, ravenous larvae surrounded by a generous sprinkling of frass, the politically and entomologically correct term for caterpillar waste. The tent keeps pace with the growth of its inhabitants; the caterpillars continue to add to it over the course of a season until it is nearly a foot or more in length.

Eastern tent caterpillars begin their lives as eggs packed in shiny dark brown packets wrapped around twigs of the food plant. Each packet contains as many as 150 to 350 eggs and is sufficiently insulated to protect the eggs from the killing frosts of winter.

The gregarious caterpillars hatch with the first flush of leaf growth, and gather to spin a communal tent with specialized salivary glands. The tent protects the caterpillars from the ravages of predators, parasites, and weather. They leave the safety of the tent during the day to feed, but return home at night or during cool or rainy weather.

After about four to six weeks, the caterpillars attain maturity, reaching a length of about two inches. Their black bodies sport a yellowish white racing stripe down the back and are sparsely clothed with long, soft, light brown hairs. Eye-catching sky blue patches of scales adorn their flanks, surrounded by fine reticulations of yellow and brown.

Mature caterpillars stop feeding and abandon the security of their tents in search of a protected place to pupate. They may travel considerable distances, wandering over vegetation, sidewalks, roads, and buildings. Their powdery whitish yellow cocoons are found in leaf litter or on tree trunks, fence posts, and the sides of houses. The light chocolate brown moths, with wingspans of up to two inches, emerge in about two weeks. A pair of white diagonal stripes on each forewing distinguishes them from other similarly colored smallish and chunky moths. Only one generation is produced each year.

Native to North America, eastern tent caterpillar populations are usually kept in check by birds, predatory insects, parasitic wasps, and disease, as well as cold or wet weather. Like other plant-feeding insects, they provide a natural pruning service that encourages seed germination by both opening up the forest floor to sunlight and fertilizing the soil with their waste.

The appearance of tent caterpillars is not necessarily cause for alarm. If abundant, the caterpillars can strip a small tree or shrub of all of its leaves, weakening but seldom killing the plant. Control is seldom necessary, but the early detection and elimination of egg packets before the caterpillars hatch is probably the most effective means of control and reduces reliance upon indiscriminate insecticides. Small tents are easily destroyed with a stick or pole, exposing the caterpillars to predators and parasites.

Life on the Edge:
Monarch Butterflies

My first batch of homespun Richmond monarch butterflies flew the coop just before Hurricane Isabel. Raised from caterpillars feeding on milkweed plants in my insect garden, they now flit by only occasionally to sip nectar from the lilac-colored blossoms of my butterfly bushes. With luck, they will soon join the ranks of millions of other monarchs all across the eastern United States, from southern Canada southward, to head south of the border for the winter.

Although they don't look it, these monarchs are quite different from their parents and their parents' parents, at least on the inside. Instead of focusing their efforts on mating and laying eggs, this generation of butterflies, the last of the season, will spend most of its time drinking nectar. The nectar is stored as fat and serves as the fuel pack that will power these burnt-orange-and-black butterballs to the mountains of central Mexico.

Monarchs are under a lot of pressure these days. In the United States and Canada, habitat destruction as a result of real estate development and agricultural expansion are transforming their habitats into sterile tracts of land fit for neither caterpillar nor butterfly.

To complicate matters, milkweeds, the sole food source of the monarch's caterpillar, are also disappearing around the country. Many milkweed species prefer to grow in disturbed soils. Along roadways, these and the nectaring plants required by the adults are subjected to continual mowing and exposure to herbicides. And there is evidence that commonly used biological-control agents designed to kill the caterpillars of moth pests, such as *Bacillus thuringiensis*, popularly known as "bt," may also kill monarchs.

Monarchs, already walking an ecological tightrope just to make it through the winter, are even more vulnerable in their overwintering sites. Their annual winter roosts, both in southern Mexico and California, have been classified as a "threatened phenomenon." In Mexico, logging activities at the monarch's overwintering grounds in Michoacan continue to chip away at the oyamel fir forests that serve as a thermal blanket protecting the monarchs from frost, rain, wind, and sunlight.

Overwintering sites along the Pacific coast are also under stress. Since the middle of the nineteenth century, overwintering California monarchs have been able to expand southward, thanks to the inadvertent creation of thermal blankets in the form of Australian eucalyptus groves. The trees were originally planted as cheap sources of lumber and as windbreaks.

But now real estate development and agricultural expansion threaten to pull the blanket off, exposing countless butterflies to the winter elements. Although the largest known overwintering sites are protected within state parks, the continual loss of adjacent smaller sites limits the food and shelter available to the butterflies throughout the winter.

It's hard to imagine that such a spectacular, ubiquitous insect could ever be in trouble. Still, I decided to do my bit by planting an insect garden this past spring, including three milkweed plants, to provide a tiny oasis for local monarchs and other insects. After all these years, the promise and fact of witnessing the marvel of monarch metamorphosis still fills me with giddy anticipation and awe.

To find out more about monarch biology and conservation, milkweed growing tips, research involving student\scientist part-

nerships, and tagging projects, visit http://www.monarchwatch
.org/.

Out on a Limb:
Fall Webworms

Take a long drive across Virginia's interstates or a short walk along
her wooded footpaths during the months of August and September; on either trip you're bound to spot the protective silken enclosures of the fall webworm, *Hyphantria cunea*. Native to North
America, the fall webworm is the caterpillar stage of a moth and
is responsible for the unsightly webs on up to one hundred different kinds of deciduous forest, orchard, and ornamental trees.
Walnut, elm, hickory, box elder, sweet gum, maples, and various
fruit trees are all leaves of choice for webworms living in eastern
United States.

Unlike the tent caterpillars, which set up their bivouacs in the
crotches of branches, fall webworms set up housekeeping on the
leaf-bearing branch tips. There is seldom cause for concern since
the damage occurs late in the season, just before the host trees
are due to drop their leaves anyway. They usually confine their
feeding activities to leaves inside their tents, leaving much of the
tree unaffected. The webs are considered to be more of an aesthetic problem than a pest infestation in parks and neighborhoods.
However, small trees may be stripped completely of their leaves
and die when attacked by hundreds of voracious larvae.

The adult moth is pure white or nearly so, with a wingspan
of less than two inches. Emerging from their cocoons from May
through July, the moths soon mate and lay masses of two hundred
or more yellow or light green eggs on the undersides of leaves,
often near the tips of the branches. The female partially covers
the egg masses with a defensive coating of hairlike scales from her
own body.

The hatchlings immediately spin protective nests or tents
around their leafy food. The tents are small at first, but grow
quickly to keep pace with their growing and ravenous inhabitants.

The tents are filled with the lacey and skeletonized remains of leaves, caterpillars, and their excrement. The caterpillars vary in color, from pale yellow to green, with a broad, dusky stripe down their back and a yellowish stripe on each side. They are covered in long, silky gray tufts that originate on orange-yellow or black tubercles. Young larvae merely graze on the upper surfaces of the leaves, while older caterpillars strip the leaves of all their tissues, leaving behind only the midrib and major veins.

The hairy-looking caterpillars are gregarious until they reach their final stage of growth, after which the inch-long larvae may be found individually wandering about their food plant. When fully grown, these solitary feeders begin migrating down the trunks of trees to spin a cocoon and pupate in the leaf litter, under bark, and in old nest remains. They remain in the pupal stage through the winter, emerging the following spring.

Though fall webworms are unsightly, the damage they cause is generally insignificant. While birds generally avoid eating fall webworms because of their irritating hairs, nearly ninety species of naturally occurring insect parasitoids and predators are known to attack the larvae in the United States. Ichneumon and braconid wasps parasitize the caterpillars, while predators such as paper wasps, yellow jackets, hornets, and stink bugs prey on the webworms. When control is necessary, pruning and destroying larval webs as soon as they are discovered can be effective, especially for smaller trees.

For All You Moth-ers Out There!

A little over a month ago, I joined other insect enthusiasts to participate in Virginia's first "Bugathon," near Vontay in Hanover County. Our goal was to find as many different kinds of insects as possible during a twenty-hour period.

Our host, Chris Ludwig, chief biologist of the Virginia Division of Natural Heritage, set his sights on the moths. For nearly seven years, he has spent more than five hundred nights on his property lurking around lights and inspecting sweet, fruity baits in search of these primarily nocturnal creatures. He has turned up 537 species thus far.

Both moths and butterflies belong to the order Lepidoptera, a group of insects characterized by a coating of scales on their wings that overlap like the shingles on a roof. Technically, most moths possess a structure that links their fore- and hind wings together, while butterflies lack this linkage. Moths are generally active at night, more heavy bodied, and somberly hued. The key word here is "usually" since there are many butterflylike moths. When in doubt, check out the antennae. In moths, they are threadlike or feathery. In butterflies, the antennae are swollen or hooked at the tips.

Of the estimated 130,000 lepidopterans around the world, only about 10 percent are butterflies. Approximately 2,700 species of moths and 168 species of butterflies occur in the commonwealth. Although clearly in the majority, moths tend to get a bum rap among the public because they are considered "creatures of the dark." The fact that the immature stages of a few species nibble on or destroy things we value doesn't help their cause either.

For example, the caterpillars of clothes moths and Indian meal moths nibble woolen sweaters and destroy stored pantry products, respectively. Corn earworms ravage kernels still on the stalk, while tomato hornworms the size of sausages devour the leaves of tomatoes, peppers, and eggplants. And the larvae of some species, such as the carpenterworm, bore into the trunks of hardwoods and reduce the value of managed timber.

But a couple of moth larvae have captured our attention in a positive way and have found their way into commerce. Silkworms are not only our primary source of silk, they are also raised in schools everywhere to provide students with lessons in both silk production and metamorphosis. And small beanlike fruits infested with twitchy caterpillars are often sold as novelty items and are known as Mexican jumping beans.

The vast majority of moths remain unsung heroes of the natural world as they pollinate flowers and provide juicy morsels for hungry bats, birds, and countless other insect-eating animals. Some Virginia moths rival butterflies in their beauty, but even the drabber species are draped in pleasing earth-toned patterns.

You can see moths at porch lights or storefronts almost any-time of year in Virginia. Moths, like other nocturnal insects, orient themselves by using ultraviolet rays, hence their attraction to lights. Warm spring and summer nights are usually best, especially on dark, moonless nights. On these same nights, heavily perfumed garden flowers, such as evening primroses, lure in dozens of these scaly-winged nocturnal pollinators, some of them the size of hummingbirds. As they hover about the flowers, the moths unfurl their long tongues to sip the sweet nectar from deep inside the blooms.

Moth watching anyone?

To learn more about moths, visit http://www.butterfliesand moths.org/.

Tales of Mulberries and Moths

With the imminent arrival of spring, science teachers across the commonwealth will find themselves scrambling through neighborhoods and parks in search of leafy mulberry trees. The leaves produced by the trees will become feasts for hungry silkworms, caterpillars of the silk moth, *Bombyx mori*. The green and leafy fodder will soon be transformed into silk. Although spiders and a variety of insects produce silk, most commercial silk is harvested from the cocoons spun by silkworms. A native of China, silkworms are the world's only completely domesticated insects; none are known in the wild.

As they feed, the freshly hatched silkworms will increase their body weight ten thousand times and reach three inches in length in just six weeks before spinning their silken cocoons. Each cocoon consists of a single silken thread up to three thousand feet long. It takes about 1,700 cocoons or 125 pounds of mulberry leaves to make one silk dress. Just one pound of caterpillars can consume twelve tons of leaves before reaching the pupal stage.

Sericulture, or the raising of silkworms and harvesting of their silk, dates back to 2600 BC. Raw silk eventually became an important trade item between China and Europe. Venetian traveler Marco Polo followed trade routes collectively known as the Silk Road on his epic journey to China in the thirteenth century. The Silk Road stretched eastward from the northeastern shore of the Mediterranean Sea across Iraq and Turkistan into China.

For centuries, the Chinese carefully guarded the secrets of the silk industry, but in about 555 AD, monks living in China who were savvy to silkworms smuggled eggs and plants back to the West. Until 1865, all the silkworms in Europe and the United States were the direct descendants of these ill-gotten gains.

England briefly participated in the silk trade, using its North American colonies as a base of operations. By 1614, sericulture was successfully under way in Virginia. The planting of ten mulberry trees for every one hundred acres became the law of the land, and fines extracted in the form of tobacco were levied against those who failed to comply. Numerous pamphlets appeared extolling the profits of silkworm culture; mulberry bark was touted for its use in the manufacture of linens and rope, and the leaves were advertised as swine food. The industry expanded in the Carolinas and Georgia, but colonists found that growing tobacco was more profitable than raising silkworms. By 1760, sericulture began to decline steadily in the colonies.

Because they are fed and raised in close quarters, silkworms are highly susceptible to various pathogens. During some of the early investigations of one of these diseases, Louis Pasteur correctly deduced the microbial origin of disease. The rest, as they say, is history.

China and Japan remain the largest modern producers of silk, with China accounting for about 80 percent of the world's raw silk production. Japan is one of the world's largest consumers of silk, a market driven by the manufacture of kimonos. Italy is the largest producer of silk in Europe, while the United States is by far the world's largest importer.

Knots of hungry silkworms on beds of mulberry leaves are

common fixtures in today's middle-school classrooms. Raising these eating machines not only provides lessons in history and commerce but also affords an up-close-and-personal look at one of nature's most fascinating phenomena, metamorphosis. The transformation of tiny eggs into caterpillars, cocoons, and moths has and will be fixed in the minds of generations of students.

Question Marks Punctuate the First Warm Days of Spring

Butterflies have often been compared fancifully to flowers. They are certainly like them in that each kind has its own season for appearing in perfect bloom.

—Samuel Hubbard Scudder, *Everyday Butterflies* (1899)

I was sitting on my favorite rock jutting out into the James River the other day, watching dozens of herring gulls circling over the water. They landed and scuffled with one another for tiny bits of real estate on the flat, dry rocks that barely peeked out above the water's surface. Double-crested cormorants beat their wings high overhead, rushing off to who knows where. And, invisible against the trees lining the shore, I could hear the harsh rattle of a not-so-distant belted kingfisher.

There were hints of spring all around me as I soaked up the hazy, late morning sunshine. Soft clumps of green moss and grass dotted the riverbank. Leaf buds swelled up and down the branches of trees and shrubs lining the water. Even the newly unfurled leaves of the common briar, nature's barbed wire, were, for the moment anyway, a welcome sight after another winter's worth of grays and browns.

Suddenly, a flash of burnt orange darted over the water just in front of me. It quickly retreated back to shore and landed on a nearby red maple trunk. The tree's branches were dressed in thousands of tiny, delicate red flowers. I slowly approached the tree, hoping to get a better look, but the source of the flash of color was gone. Or was it?

With its wings closed, the ragged wing margins and nearly uniformly brownish gray tones on the underside of this butterfly made it look as if it were a dead leaf growing straight out of the bark. The silver crescent and dot at the center of the hind wing suggested a punctuation mark. This vernal sprite was a question mark butterfly—my first for the season!

This early spring speedster had carefully chosen its perch, a patch of trunk drenched in both sun and sap. A small, bubbly flow was forced out of a wound by the spate of warm weather. With its long and coiled proboscis unfurled, the butterfly appeared as though it were using a soda straw to suck up the fluid. Unlike many butterflies, question marks seldom seek nectar-bearing flowers for a meal. Instead, they prefer to visit sap flows, fresh dung, carrion, rotting fruit, and mud for their nutrients.

As it sipped, the butterfly began to slowly pump its wings, occasionally revealing the burnt orange upper side of its wings, all speckled with black spots. Each wing was trimmed with a narrow band of gray with more than a hint of violet. Each hind wing had a small, yet distinct tail. Apparently satiated, the question mark suddenly bolted into the woods.

On the wing, both male and female question marks always seem to be in a hurry. Males are quite territorial and stake out trees, rocks, or patches of ground to wait for passing females. Males looking for love are quite aggressive and will attempt to chase away intruders of all sizes and species from their pickup spots.

Question marks are among the first butterflies on the wing each year. Because they overwinter as adults, they are fully winged and raring to go on the occasional warm, sunny days that punctuate the wintery months of January and February. By late March, the fits and starts of spring regularly drive these insects out of their winter hideaways under bark, inside tree holes, or among stacks of firewood. With the full-on arrival of spring, question marks are a common sight throughout all of eastern United States.

Females lay their pale green eggs, up to eight at a time, on the undersides of leaves in the elm and nettle plant families. During the last half of May, the first caterpillars begin to hatch. Variable in color, these striped and sexless eating machines are all well armed with rows of prickly tubercles. When threatened, these future butterflies curl up to protect the vulnerable heads and underbellies of their presently wormlike bodies. This behavior presents their attackers with a bristling array of spines pointing outward in all directions, an uncomfortable mouthful for even the hungriest of birds.

There are at least two generations of question marks produced annually in Virginia. The last generation of butterflies emerges in late August. They will remain on the wing through the last warm days of November before seeking places to hibernate. The upper hind wing surfaces of the summer generation are nearly black, while those appearing in fall and spring are more orange with black spots. The lower surface of the wings varies in both broods. They are nearly uniform in color, or striated with fine, wavy brown lines, and may or may not be tinged in violet.

Question marks are widespread in Virginia and haunt a variety of habitats—open deciduous woods, brushy thickets, damp fields, and forest glades. They are especially evident along river and stream banks, trails and roadsides, and they sometimes grace bushy gardens and wooded parks with their presence. Question marks in daily evidence are a clear indication that winter has finally passed and the full weight of spring will soon be upon us.

Learn more about butterflies from the Butterfly Society of Virginia at http://www.butterflysocietyofva.org/.

4

Bodacious

Beetles

Everyone has, or should have, a passion; mine is beetles. I am, and always will be, a beetle man. They have been one of the most important and consistent driving forces in my life for more than thirty years, ever since my sophomore year in high school. Yet, sometimes the hold they have on me is somewhat of a mystery. I still have not yet been able to fully articulate what it is about beetles that they preoccupy so much of my waking hours each day. Yet, more often than not, the promise of beetles, literally or figuratively, is what drives me out of bed nearly every day and sends me out on a quest to see, learn, and do more. I even dream about them, especially in the wintertime, when my contacts with them are decidedly limited to photos of past encounters or dead specimens on pins. In my dreams I can identify the beetles to genus, but the species of my dreams are twice as big and colorful as they are in real life and hanging low on trees and shrubs as if they were fruit.

I await their emergence every spring with the same enthusiasm with which one would greet an old friend not seen in a very long time. I find something very comforting about the fact that they appear so regularly, year after year. This annual cycle somehow gives me a sense of purpose and comfort in an all-too-chaotic universe. And they awaken within me something very primal—I suppose it might be likened to the thrill and excitement of the hunt—as I stalk them along riverbanks, wooded paths, and graveled alleys. These days, I usually undertake these safaris with a camera in hand; my "take" is generally limited to capturing their likenesses on film.

Ever since I can remember, I have always been enamored with

their hard, compact bodies and their seemingly infinite variety of colors and behaviors. My fascination with their form and function is fueled by the fact that they are found virtually everywhere. And I have been very fortunate to follow the activities of these amazingly diverse animals in several parts of the world, including Mexico, Costa Rica, Kenya, Malawi, Namibia, and South Africa.

But when it comes to beetles and other insects, you don't have to be a world traveler to take in exotic sights and sounds; your experience can begin right here at home. Across the United States, from the xeric desert dunes of southeastern California to the mesic mountain forests in the Great Smokies of Tennessee, there is a breathtaking array of beetles just waiting to be discovered and studied by the most dedicated of scientists, or observed and enjoyed by the casual naturalist. Virginia alone is home to perhaps some six thousand species of beetles, most of which are poorly known in terms of their distributions and natural histories. Whether you live in the city or country, new discoveries in the world of beetles are virtually guaranteed. I am convinced that beetle study practiced by carefully observing them in the wild, capturing their images on film or computer, making a collection, or bringing them back alive and rearing them in the classroom provides the most fortunate of us with a lifetime of exploration, discovery, and wonder.

The Age of Beetles

Beetles live almost everywhere. A few inhabit the narrow fringes of the polar ice caps, while most dwell in the ever-dwindling rain forests. Coleopterists, scientists who study beetles, have catalogued approximately 350,000 species around the world. They are the personification of biodiversity; one out of five of every plant and animal species is a beetle. And if sheer numbers of species were a criterion for success, then beetles would surely have to be the most successful animals on Earth.

Beetles are tiny recycling machines, devouring plants, animals, and their remains. Although some species are considered serious pests (e.g., Japanese beetles, bark beetles, and boll weevils), most are absolutely essential to a smoothly operating ecosystem. In fact, the presence or absence of some beetles, especially aquatic species, is used as a measure of environmental health.

Beetles are designed to go the distance. The highly specialized bodies of beetles have permitted them to occupy a staggering array of habitats with relative ease. Small and compact, beetles are incredibly well equipped to hide, burrow, eat, reproduce, and lay their eggs in virtually every terrestrial and freshwater environment, thanks to their ability to live in places and spaces often left unoccupied by other animals. And the power of flight allows many beetles to escape from predators, find mates, and locate food.

Like all insects and their relatives, the hard outer shell of beetles, or exoskeleton, functions as both skin and skeleton. Scattered about the exoskeleton are hairlike setae, structures that connect the beetle to its environment, transmitting information directly to the nervous system. Dense patches of setae also reduce the amount of abrasion caused by burrowing in wood and soil, as well functioning as a dry lubricant between moving body parts. Horns and spines discourage predators, while waxy secretions help to retain moisture. And like our own bodies, the beetle skeleton provides a support system for powerful muscles.

The first pair of the beetle's wings, or elytra, is thick and leathery. Elytra are unique to beetles. They protect the membranous flight wings and internal organs from abrasion and injury as they move, burrow, and bore through their habitats. And these tough, shell-like structures help to shield beetles from the ravages of predators, parasites, dehydration, and extreme temperatures.

For example, the space between the elytra and the abdomen insulates desert beetles from extreme temperatures and minimizes water loss through respiration. And this same cavity provides aquatic beetles with a place to trap a bubble of air so they can breathe while submerged.

It seems logical that the possession of protective and versatile elytra is a beetle's ticket to success. However, this hypothesis is difficult to test scientifically, so researchers have begun to look for other ways to explain the amazing diversity of beetles. Since over half of all beetles are plant feeders, Harvard entomologist Brian Farrell examined the evolutionary relationship between beetles and plants to better understand the reasons behind beetle diversity. Fortunately for Farrell and others, the structures of beetles and plants are durable and frequently preserved in the fossil record, giving researchers the opportunity to examine evolutionary trends through time.

The earliest-known fossil beetles are approximately 230 million years old and are believed to have dined on dead organic material and fungi. Fossil evidence indicates that plant feeding among beetles arose 50 million years later, about the time of the appearance of gymnosperms (pines and other conifers), cycads, and gingkoes.

Late in the Cretaceous period, approximately 65 million years ago, about the time dinosaurs began to disappear, the first flowering plants, or angiosperms, appeared. Angiosperms provided beetles with a new, underexploited resource. Already adept at utilizing vegetative structures, the beetle's shift from gymnosperms to angiosperms was relatively simple. Roots, stems, leaves, flowers, and fruits not only provided food, they also offered shelter for immature and adult beetles alike, increasing their ecological opportunities to prosper and diversify.

The crucible of plant-beetle interactions has tested the mettle of these two groups for millions of years and continues today. Just as the increasing diversity of angiosperms put beetles on an evolutionary fast track, angiosperms themselves continued to diversify, developing new defenses against the unrelenting pressure of beetle attacks. Beetles and flowering plants had to adapt to one another or die. Over time, this "rumba" resulted in the overall success of both beetles and flowering plants.

The life cycle of most beetles is divided into four distinct stages—egg, larva, pupa, and adult. This type of development, known as complete metamorphosis, is shared with butterflies, moths, flies, ants, bees, wasps, and even fleas. With different environmental and nutritional requirements, larval and adult beetles function in the environment as two completely different animals. This arrangement avoids potentially harmful competition for food and space among generations.

Female beetles either carefully deposit single eggs on or near suitable foodstuffs, or they may scatter hundreds of them about haphazardly. Upon hatching, the larva's sole job is to eat. Depending upon the species, beetle larvae scavenge carrion, consume animal excrement, attack roots, mine through leaves, chew their way through wood, or hunt for living prey. The pupal stage marks the transition between larva and adult. It is during this stage that the tissues of a nonreproductive eating machine are transformed into a precision breeding instrument that may or may not require food.

The ancient Egyptians were fascinated by dung-rolling scarabs and had some knowledge of their life cycles, observing that every year these industrious creatures buried balls of dung, giving rise to more beetles. They interpreted the activities of these beetles to represent their own world in miniature. The ancient Egyptian sun god Ra was symbolized as a great scarab rolling the sun, like a dung ball, across the heavens. The burying of the dung ball symbolized the rising and setting of the sun. Some scholars have suggested that the ancient Egyptians' knowledge of the scarab's metamorphic processes, including the mummylike pupa formed within the buried dung ball, may have inspired human mummification within underground chambers. Images of sacred scarabs appeared everywhere. Carved scarabs bore religious inscriptions or simple wishes for good luck, health, and life. Heart scarabs were placed on or near the chest of the mummy and bore inscriptions admonishing the heart not to bear witness against its own master on judgment day.

In spite of their adaptability and evolutionary success, beetles are not immune to environmental pressures and habitat loss. Urbanization, fire, and acid rain all reduce their populations. Electric lights create unnatural concentrations of beetles and expose them to hungry predators. Bug zappers, sold as a form of insect control, needlessly kill many beetles and countless other insects. Overgrazing, agricultural practices, water impoundment, pollution, deforestation, soil erosion, off-road recreational vehicles, and logging all take a heavy toll on beetle communities. Only through habitat preservation and the careful surveying of beetle populations can we begin to understand their role in our own quality of life.

The familiar yet bizarre nature of beetles makes them the perfect ambassadors for environmental awareness. Fascination with the behavior, color, and form of beetles can fuel a lifelong passion for all living things. Through this passion we acknowledge our interdependence with nature, enhancing not only our lives but also the lives of those around us.

Find out more about beetles at the Coleopterists Society Web site at http://www.coleopsoc.org.

Eastern Hercules Beetles: Armed, but Not Dangerous

Some people find their first eastern Hercules beetle in a parking lot on a muggy summer morning lying on its back clawing at the air with dark, powerful legs. Harmless to people and pets, many of these hapless top-heavy creatures soon succumb to the broiling sun or crushing vehicular traffic. But a few lucky individuals manage to be rescued by curious and sympathetic onlookers.

Hercules beetles are one of the largest beetles in the eastern United States. Males are equipped with a short, up-curved horn mounted on their heads and are sometimes called rhino beetles. Their midsection sports a longer horn flanked by two small spines. The horns are used in battle with other males. Females are not so adorned. Although males measure 1.5 to 2.5 inches from horn to stern, they pale in comparison to their tropical cousins that reach nearly 7 inches, much of it horn.

Each wing cover has a background color of brownish black and is covered with an irregular layer of yellow green or gray. The blotchy or speckled pattern of each beetle is distinctive, like fingerprints. Occasionally one wing cover is mottled while the other is a uniform brownish black. As the beetles imbibe fluids, their wing covers may become entirely dark.

Adults emerge in June and July and remain active through September. During their nocturnal ramblings, Hercules beetles are frequently lured to streetlights and well-lit storefronts. They announce their presence with a powerful buzz as they fly and land with a resounding thud. By day they are found feeding on the sap of ash trees but are occasionally attracted to rotting fruit. In captivity they may live several weeks on a solution of maple syrup and water soaked in a cotton ball interspersed with an occasional slice of apple, banana, peach, pear, or plum.

In the wild, males stake out sap flows on ash trees and wait for the arrival of a potential mate. Other males are greeted with the pincerlike horns. The rival beetles grapple with one another until one of them gives up the fight or is knocked to the ground. Battles between rival males seldom result in serious injury or death among the combatants.

In August, the females seek out tree holes in mature oaks or other trees, where they lay their eggs. For nearly two years, the C-shaped grubs feed on the rotten, woody bits that have accumulated in the cavity, but they pose no harm to the living tree.

When ready to pupate, each grub constructs a protective cell about the size of a tennis ball. The cell wall is made up of bits of wood and their own waste. Adults emerge from their pupae in fall but remain inactive inside their cells until the following summer.

Fortunately some Hercules beetles still manage to eke out a living among the ever-expanding tracts of treeless land that make up our neighborhoods and parks. Their welcome presence is yet another reminder that little bits of wildness can still be found here and there within the greater environs of Richmond.

Beetles Must Bark Up the Right Tree for Winter

Winter may seem like the death knell for all insects. And for many individuals, shorter days and freezing nights do mark the end of the road, at least for the adults. But don't despair. The six-legged borers, grazers, scavengers, and hunters of Virginia's spring and summer are still around. They have simply hunkered down in a less conspicuous life stage to ride out the winter.

To beat the freeze, many insects spend the winter as eggs, larvae, or pupae—developmental stages better suited for surviving sustained, chilly temperatures. Cold-hardy adults tuck themselves away deep in the soil or wedge themselves in the nooks and crannies afforded by trees.

As a result of the force and fury of Hurricane Isabel, I was afforded a bird's-eye view of some beetles that usually spend their winters ten or more feet above the ground, sandwiched in the tight spaces between the bark and sound wood of standing dead trees.

Living in total darkness, these beetles feed on creeping sheets of fungus or prey on other fungus feeders. They meet the physical challenges of little or no headroom by growing no more than a few millimeters and/or having almost paper-thin profiles.

Teardrop-shaped rove beetles of the genus *Coproporus* (Latin scholars will appreciate the derivation of this scientific appellation) are just a few millimeters long and resemble tiny black horseshoe crabs. They slip easily under the bark, searching for plump, juicy mites and other small invertebrates.

Flat, rectangular hister beetles of the genus *Hololepta* and their relatives look like shiny black bits of patent leather equipped with short, sharp mandibles. They too feast on tiny insects, mites, and their eggs.

One of the most spectacular denizens of these tight spaces is the fire-engine-red flat bark beetle, *Cucujus flavipes.* Flat bark beetles are common under the bark of both conifers and hardwoods throughout eastern North America. However, little is known of their biology. Super flat, this ¾-inch beetle is a relative giant among its peers.

The broad, flat, yellowish brown larvae of flat bark beetles also live under bark and are heavily armored and distinctly segmented, resembling a Lilliputian bracelet with legs. They outnumber the adults during the winter months and are better able to beat the cold thanks to high levels of chemicals in their bodies that function as antifreeze. These chemicals inhibit the formation of deadly, razor-sharp ice crystals inside their cells that would expand and shred the cell walls, reducing their muscles and organs to mush.

Surprisingly, standing dead wood is a rapidly disappearing habitat. Ill-informed land managers around the commonwealth have used Hurricane Isabel and other natural disasters that down numerous trees as an excuse to clear trees from parks and other lands, dead and otherwise. Old, hollow trees with thin crowns put up little resistance to high winds and are less likely than their younger, solid counterparts to be knocked down by hurricane-force winds. And the possession of dead, unsafe limbs is never an environmentally sound reason for cutting down an entire tree.

The removal of these trees, especially those that pose no threat to property or people, leaves countless invertebrates, reptiles, and amphibians out in the cold. Come spring, already depressed populations of woodpeckers and other tree-hole nesting birds will have to contend with even fewer sites to raise their young. These sylvan high-rises, with their permanent sap flows, hollows, splits, weather-damaged branches, bracket fungi, and other imperfections, are important havens for a mind-boggling array of life and are worthy of our attention, concern, and protection.

Counting Tigers on Virginia's Eastern Shore

The bright colors, bulging eyes, big jaws, and lightning-fast reflexes of tiger beetles have never failed to grab attention or inspire admiration. Voracious predators all, they pounce on many different kinds of insects, running down their small prey and cutting them to pieces with their scythelike mandibles. Twenty species of tiger beetles call Virginia home, where they are often found scurrying along waterways and beaches, sun-dappled trails, and woodland openings.

Probably the best known of all Virginia species is the northeastern beach tiger beetle, *Cicindela dorsalis dorsalis.* Although relatively common in Virginia, these tiger beetles have not been so fortunate elsewhere in their range. Once a common sight along the open beaches of the northeastern Atlantic coast from Cape Cod to southern New Jersey, they are known today only from a few populations on the Atlantic at Martha's Vineyard and a few other localities in Massachusetts.

Their coastal breeding grounds are nothing more than a narrow ribbon of real estate hugging the water's edge. It was inevitable that their populations beyond the eastern and western shores of Chesapeake Bay would begin to crash as a direct result of heavy vehicular and foot beach traffic. This precipitous decline, coupled with the possibility of development that threatened Maryland and Virginia beetle populations around the Chesapeake, led to the beetle's listing as threatened by the United States Fish and Wildlife Service in 1990.

Today, thanks to a coalition of federal, state, and other agencies, these fleet-footed animals now enjoy the summer sun in Virginia and elsewhere without the threat of crushing pedestrian and vehicular beach traffic, or the ravages of unchecked development.

I wanted to see these tiger beetles up close and headed out to the Savage Neck Dunes Natural Area Preserve. Owned and managed by the Virginia Department of Conservation and Recreation, Division of Natural Heritage, this 299-acre preserve was set aside, in part, as a refuge for the northeastern beach tiger beetles. Here they seem to thrive along an undisturbed mile-long section of the Chesapeake Bay shoreline.

The preserve also includes a variety of coastal habitats, including pristine maritime forest, dune shrub, and grassland communities. The Savage Neck dunes, for which the preserve is named, are piled nearly fifty feet high, making it one of the highest points on the Delmarva Peninsula.

The Virginia Natural Area Preserve System was established in the late 1980s to protect some of Virginia's most significant natural areas. Around the state these preserves include examples of some of the commonwealth's rare plant communities and sensitive species habitats.

At the preserve, just past the long-fallow agricultural fields, are towering oaks, red maples, sweet gums, loblolly pines, and hollies. The woodland floor is covered here and there with formidable tangles of common greenbrier. Their tough vines look and function like barbed wire with chlorophyll. They tugged at my boots and tore mercilessly into my pant legs as I made my way west to the beach.

As I got closer to the Chesapeake Bay, the forest overhead opened up to reveal low, gnarled shrubs rooted in soft, white sand. Struggling to survive in this nutrient-poor soil, many of these plants were stunted versions of their more statuesque inland counterparts. But a few species seem to thrive here; they were dune specialists and prefer to grow nowhere else but in sandy soils.

The scattered shrubs quickly gave way to clumps of American beach and coastal panic grasses. These resilient and salt-resistant grasses disappear entirely on the nearly flat, open beach. From here to the warm, clear water quietly lapping on shore were chunks of driftwood and mats of rotting eelgrass, punctuated by the occasional dead fish, seashells, small polished stones, and other various bits of debris all human in origin.

Standing on the shoreline and squinting in the bright sun, the humid, still air was stifling, wrapping itself around my sweaty face and body like an electrical blanket set on high. Every now and again the slightest hint of breeze came off the bay, briefly offering the empty promise of a slightly less oppressive afternoon.

This is exactly the kind of day that northeastern beach tiger beetles live for. Scanning the waterline, I could see them by the dozens running along the moist sand at the water's edge, dressed in an almost ghostly shade of white. Their pale coloration helps them to blend in with the white sand and also helps to deflect some of the intense sunlight.

From June through August, the beetles begin their day by basking in the sun on the loose, dry sand along the back beach. As the day warms they move toward the cooler, wetter sands along the water's edge to cool off by "stilting," raising their heads high, appearing as if they were standing on the tips of all six of their toes.

This seemingly haughty posture is really quite practical. It reduces the horizontal surface of their body exposed to the sun's blistering rays, lifts their head and thorax above the warm layer of air hugging the sand, and minimizes their exposure to the stultifying heat reflected from the hot sand beneath.

Their entire life cycle is played out along a narrow strip of shoreline wedged between the water's edge to no more than just a few feet beyond the high-tide mark. Long, broad beaches with lots of open, loose sand create the ideal habitat for these tiger beetles. Artificially stabilized shorelines are of little or no use because they don't have sand with the necessary properties. Narrow beaches with lots of foot and vehicular traffic are especially lethal to sedentary larvae that are absolutely dependent upon stable habitats.

Restricted to vertical burrows in the sand, the larvae must endure and survive not one but two winters before reaching maturity. They occupy an area from the midintertidal zone to several feet above the high-tide line, a habitat ranging from nine to twenty-four feet wide. Beach hoppers are abundant here and are the primary source of food for hungry beetle larvae.

Although thousands of beetles may be found at the height of the season at the preserve, most populations are considerably smaller and live on unprotected, privately owned tracts of beach. Fortunately, these habitats are generally inaccessible to heavy pedestrian and vehicular traffic, which is good news for the beetles.

However, adults do fall victim to hungry robber flies and wolf spiders, while a parasitoid wasp attacks the larvae in their burrows. Nevertheless the tiger beetles are better able to deal with these natural hazards than those inflicted upon them by human beachgoers.

I spent two afternoons watching these pale and leggy predators charge up and down their sandy strip of real estate, keeping just ahead of the constantly shifting tides as they searched for food and mates. I also helped to count thousands of them as part of a regular census conducted by the staff of the Division of Natural Heritage. I will always remain in awe of the northeastern beach tiger beetle, marveling at its ability to make do under some of the most difficult of conditions, with and without our help.

To learn more about tiger beetles, see *A Field Guide to the Tiger Beetles of the United States and Canada,* by David L. Pearson, C. Barry Knisley, and Charles J. Kazilek (2006).

For information and photos of Virginia tiger beetles, visit http://www.npwrc.usgs.gov/resource/distr/insects/tigb/va/toc.htm.

Invasion of the Body Snatchers

The late-morning air was thick from the previous night's heavy summer downpour. The pungent aroma of rotting fish laid out earlier had begun to work its magic, drawing in wave after wave of ants, flies, and wasps. Even hackberry butterflies dined on the putrid flesh, sucking up mineral-laden fluids with their unfurled, strawlike mouthparts. And soon, the American carrion beetles, *Necrophila americana,* began to arrive, flying low over the ground in ever-tighter circles as they tracked the plume of odor to the remains.

The midsection of these handsome, ¾-inch beetles is bright yellow with a large black spot in the middle. Their dull black wing covers are broadly oval, faintly ribbed, and roughly textured. In flight they look like flat, slow-flying bumblebees as they search woodlands and fields for dead vertebrates. They presumably acquire some degree of protection from predators by mimicking a large, stinging bee.

The American carrion beetle is widespread throughout the eastern half of the United States and southern Canada. Adults overwinter and begin mating in late spring through early summer. Eggs are laid in the soil in the vicinity of a carcass and develop into adults in about ten to twelve weeks. Both adults and larvae feed on soft, decaying flesh and its excretions, but the larvae seem particularly fond of the bits of dried tissue left behind by maggots.

Carrion beetles and other insect scavengers break down remains of dead animals into their most basic components, recycling them so they are once again available for use by other living things. A few carrion beetles are also drawn to dung or fungi, where they prey on insects, while others are known to nibble on plants. A European species was introduced into the northeastern United States to eat gypsy moth caterpillars, but it never became established.

There are about 175 species of carrion beetles worldwide, all classified under the family Silphidae. Of the thirty species of silphids living in North America north of Mexico, eleven occur in Virginia. The majority of silphids are gray or dull black, but some have bright yellow, orange, or red markings. The Silphidae is further subdivided into two subfamilies, the Silphinae and Nicrophorinae.

The Silphinae, including the American carrion beetles, lay their eggs just beneath a carcass that has already begun to decompose. The eggs hatch in four to five days, and the larvae begin feeding immediately on the decaying flesh, along with the rest of their other competitors. The long, smooth, black larvae molt three times before pupating in a chamber in the soil.

Famous for their habit of burying small vertebrate carcasses beneath the surface of the soil, the Nicrophorinae are also known as burying, or sexton, beetles. In the not-so-distant past, every church had a sexton, or church caretaker, who provided a number of services, from ringing church bells and sweeping out the pews to grave digging. It is this last task that suggested the name of these fascinating beetles.

Jean Henri Fabre, a French naturalist who meticulously studied insect behavior and eloquently recorded his observations in the late nineteenth and early twentieth centuries, was known for making the humble exciting and the repulsive interesting. He noted that *Nicrophorus,* a genus of burying beetle also found in the United States, was different than the rest of the "cadaveric mob." "In honour of his exalted functions" Fabre writes, "he bears a red tuft at the tip of his antennae; his breast is covered with nankeen; and across his wing-cases he wears a double, scalloped scarf of vermillion. An elegant, almost sumptuous costume, very superior to that of the others, but yet lugubrious, as befits your undertaker's man."

Burying beetles of the genus *Nicrophorus* exhibit the most advanced parental behavior known in beetles, providing food and care for their young until they are ready to pupate. Either the male or female initiates the carrion-burying process and is soon joined by a mate. Carcasses contaminated with fly eggs are deemed unfit by these beetles, since the hatching maggots would soon consume all of the tissue required by the adults and their larvae.

If the carcass is encountered on soil that is too hard for burial, the beetles simply move it. Lying on their backs underneath the carcass, burying beetles use their legs as levers to move it up to several feet away. Mating occurs only after the carcass is secured in its subterranean chamber, up to eight inches beneath the surface. Whether a mouse or bird, the carcass is carefully prepared by removing all fur, feathers, legs, wings, and skin. The body is then kneaded into a ball and treated with a fungicide by repeated licking to retard its decomposition.

A depression created on the upper surface of the carcass will serve as a receptacle for droplets of regurgitated tissue deposited by the parents. The heady elixir will eventually serve as food for the newly hatched larvae. Adults communicate with their offspring by rubbing their wing covers against the abdomen to produce a clearly audible chirping sound, calling the larvae to the pool of mouse or bird purée.

The American burying beetle, *Nicrophorus americanus,* is the largest carrion beetle in the United States, measuring 25 to 35 millimeters long. Listed as a federally endangered species, this beetle was once widely distributed throughout the deciduous forests of the Northeast, including Virginia. Today it is known only from Block Island, located off the coast of Rhode Island, and the westernmost fringes of its historical range in eastern Oklahoma and Texas and parts of Arkansas, Kansas, Nebraska, and South Dakota.

The dramatic reduction of the American burying beetle population was most likely caused by a combination of factors resulting from deforestation and the subsequent decline of suitable animal carcasses. Deforestation not only disrupts the immediate environment, it also causes a shift in the forest fauna. This can happen either when the quality and quantity of carrion available are directly affected, or when the amount of carrion available is reduced through increased competition by introduced scavengers.

Death and decay may be unsettling to some, but their study has important implications. Animal remains are set upon by a succession of bacteria, fungi, and insects. Weather conditions, season, size, and exposure of the remains determine their rates of decay. The occurrence of certain insect species on a carcass is dependent upon appropriate levels of decay and is reasonably predictable. This orderly progression of decay not only recycles dead tissues, it also allows forensic entomologists, scientists who study insects associated with dead bodies, to determine events surrounding the death of an individual.

Well aware of the important role that burying beetles and other insect scavengers played in the ecosystem, Fabre concluded: "They were making a clearance of death on the behalf of life. Transcendent alchemists, they were transforming that horrible putrescence into a living and inoffensive product." By interring the dead bodies of birds and small mammals, burying beetles not only play an important role in nutrient recycling, but their activities may also directly lead to the control of populations of pestiferous flies and ants that depend upon exposed carcasses for food and egg-laying sites.

For more information on American burying beetles, see http:// www-museum.unl.edu/research/entomology/endanger.htm.

Striking It Rich with Oil Beetles

While on a morning ramble in Pocahontas State Park, a lumbering, matte black beetle nearly an inch long with a distinct, antlike head appeared in the middle of the road. The short, leathery wing covers of the soft-bodied oil beetle did little to conceal its heavy, bloated abdomen. Sluggish and unwary, this beetle seemed fearless and took absolutely no notice of me as I crouched down for a closer look.

Oil beetles have good reason for going about their business with impunity. Their bodies are brimming with the blistering agent cantharidin. When molested in any way, oil beetles, like other blister beetles, dispense yellowish beads of caustic fluid through one or more of their knee joints. Armed with this potent feeding deterrent, easily hotter than the world's hottest hot sauce, blister beetles are able to repel the attacks of most predators, vertebrates and invertebrates alike.

In some species of blister beetles, only the males produce cantharidin. During copulation, these males pass along a dose of this powerful chemical to their mates, who in turn store it for their own defense. Later, the females coat their eggs with it to afford them some degree of protection as well.

Cantharidin has long been used as a remedy for all sorts of human ailments. It was prescribed to treat hydrophobia, rheumatism, gout, carbuncles, leprosy, earache, lethargy, and many other disorders. As late as the 1930s, it was available in this country as an over-the-counter preparation for the treatment of bladder infections, bedwetting, and hair restoration. Today, the blistering agent is gaining popularity in some medical circles as a wart remover.

For centuries, Europeans have ground up various blister beetle species to create a concoction known as Musae Hispanicae, or Spanishfly. A precursor to Viagra, Spanishfly was not only believed to enhance the sexual performance of men, it was also thought to increase the desires of women, too. Unfortunately, using Spanishfly to inflame passions often resulted in death from cantharidin poisoning. Just 30 milligrams of the stuff taken internally constitutes a lethal dose in humans. Because cantharidin is such an effective feeding deterrent, only a mere fraction of this amount is found in any individual beetle.

I once had a topical encounter with cantharidin. One hot, summer day in the fringes of the Mojave Desert in southern California, I came across dozens of orange and black blister beetles dangling from a patch of flowers like ripe fruit. Well aware of their blistering properties, I picked them up carefully, allowing only the tough skin on my fingertips to come harmlessly into contact with their bodies. I quickly placed them in a jar for further study and noted the yellowish stains on my fingers.

As I walked back to the car, I absentmindedly wiped the sweat from my eyes with my bare hand. Soon I became aware of a strange weight on my eyelids that seemed to shift with every step. When I arrived at my car I bent down to look at my face in the side-view mirror. My eyelids looked like a sheet of flesh-colored bubble pack. Each taut blister was filled with fluid. The blisters soon ruptured and my eyelids began to sting and burn. I carefully dabbed them with a moist tissue to avoid getting the blistering fluid into my eyes. In some cases, the area affected by cantharidin takes weeks to heal. Fortunately my discomfort lasted only several days.

Occasionally, horses and cattle accidentally swallow blister beetles while browsing or eating baled hay, resulting in a blistered mouth and tongue and severe stomach upset. Death can result from kidney failure if enough of the beetles are ingested.

The natural history of oil beetles is a wonderful mix of the films *Alien* and *Invasion of the Body Snatchers.* Their eggs are carefully laid in the soil and soon hatch into flattened, leggy, active silverfishlike larvae known as triungulins. Each triungulin crawls up a plant, settles onto a flower, and waits for a solitary, ground-nesting bee to buzz by. Stimulated by the arrival of a hairy body, the triungulin rears up and latches on to the pollinator as if it were a louse. In fact, triungulins are sometimes called bee lice. Sometimes a triungulin will latch onto the hairy, yet inappropriate body of a beetle, fly, even a honeybee. The inevitable outcome of this miscalculation is starvation and death.

The triungulin hitches a ride back to the bee's ground nest, where it disembarks to begin a new chapter of its life underground as a scavenger and parasite. Surrounded by plenty of food in the form of bee eggs, larvae, and pollen, the triungulin soon transforms itself into a series of more sedentary grubs with greatly reduced or conspicuously absent legs before reaching the pupal and adult stages. Adults emerge in spring and are active throughout the year, but the best time to see them is mid-April through June.

The courtship of oil beetles and other blister beetles is quite elaborate and includes piggyback rides, head licking, antenna pulling, and leg rubbing. Mating pairs resemble something out of Dr. Doolittle, with the pair facing in opposite directions from one another. The larvae of some species of blister beetles also attack the brood and pollen stores of ground-nesting solitary bees, or the eggs of grasshoppers.

As a group, only a few blister beetles are considered pests. The plant-feeding activities of some species focus on vegetable crops. And their presence in pastures is of concern to the owners of horses and cattle. But by and large, most species of blister beetles simply offer scientists and curious naturalists the opportunity to observe and marvel at yet another example of just how intricate and finely tuned nature can be.

5

Stings and
Wings

Ants, bees, and wasps, all members of the order Hymenoptera, are the movers and shakers in the world. As a collective, they not only help to aerate the soil and break down plant materials, they are also the primary predators and pollinators in nearly every terrestrial ecosystem. In addition, they represent a pinnacle of insect evolution because of their truly social lifestyles.

All social species live in family groups consisting of overlapping generations where labor is divided among different castes. Within these bustling colonies and hives, the worker caste performs most of the nest chores; in some species, a soldier caste is also on hand to defend the colony. Both workers and soldiers are always sterile females. The reproductives, known as queens and males (or drones), are usually the only individuals in the colony capable of reproduction. Depending on the species, queens mate anywhere from once to many times before they start a new colony. With millions of sperm tucked away for long-term storage in a special sac in their abdomens, new queens in the colony are capable of laying thousands to millions of eggs over the next five to twenty years without ever having to mate again. On the other hand, males are short-lived and die soon after they inseminate the female, their sole function in life.

In spite of the benefits of living communally, the vast majority of hymenopterans are not social at all, preferring instead to lead solitary lives. All ants are social, but most bees and wasps are loners, preferring to spend most of their lives in complete solitude.

Social or not, the most familiar aspect of hymenopterans for many people, and certainly the most excruciating, is the ability of some species to defend themselves with a painful sting. The stingers of ants, bees, and wasps are actually ovipositors, needlelike egg-laying tubes that are modified into effective defensive weapons that are capable of injecting venom. Since males have no need for oviposi-tors, they lack the necessary equipment to deliver a sting, although they will certainly probe with their abdomens as if they could.

As adults, most wasps and ants are predators, although many supplement their diets with nectar and honeydew, a sticky waste product excreted by some plant-feeding insects. But their young grow up on a steady diet of protein consisting exclusively of mac-erated or regurgitated insect or spider prey. Bees, on the other hand, consume pollen and nectar for their own sustenance and provide their young with more of the same.

A Tale of Predator and Prey

I had just spent a grueling three hours in the sweltering afternoon heat stalking insects and spiders with my camera along the James River. As I approached the Reedy Creek parking lot gate, I saw a coal-black spider wasp with equally dark wings flitting about agi-tatedly in the road. With another dozen or so exposures left in my camera, I decided to get a few pictures of the wasp before calling it a day. She flew all about me, landing briefly here and there before taking wing again. My patience quickly wore thin in the heat, and I decided that enough was enough. But then I saw what had kept the wasp in my vicinity.

Lying perfectly still and in pristine condition was a wolf spider splayed out in the middle of the road. It had been laid low by the paralyzing sting of the spider wasp and was destined to be hauled off and stuffed down a nearby burrow to become fodder for a wasp larva. I decided to stake out the living corpse right then and there in the middle of the road. Sprawled out in the rapidly fading sun, I aimed my camera at its still body in anticipation of photographing the predator with its prey.

For nearly ten minutes the wasp flew circles around me, fre-quently landing and running over the ground to search in vain for the hapless arachnid. At first I thought she was intimidated by my presence, but several times the wasp came within inches of me and my camera. Time seemed to drag on as the wasp inspected every piece of real estate in the immediate vicinity, except the tiny parcel that actually had the spider.

The occasional cyclist or jogger went past, but no one stopped to ask what I was doing. Then I heard the slow crunching of gravel coming toward me along the side of the railroad tracks. A Richmond police car slowly wheeled toward me and stopped about fifty feet away. From my perspective down on the ground, the car's headlights seemed to stare at me like two giant bug eyes separated by shiny and toothed mandibles.

I smiled in the direction of the officer and wondered what he must be thinking. Just then a big panel truck hauling a trailerload of bright blue kayaks pulled up beside me. I looked up as the driver inquired if I was all right. I assured her that I was just fine and that I was waiting to take a picture of a wasp attacking a spider. She said she hated spiders and hoped the spider would meet its demise soon and then drove off to deliver her cargo down by the river.

Then the police car pulled up. The officer told me that he did not want to ruin my shot and had decided to wait. But then he figured that if the kayak truck hadn't spoiled my shot, his police cruiser probably wouldn't either.

With all of the hubbub, I thought for sure that the wasp would have been scared off, but it was still scouring the ground in search of the spider. Finally it ran right up to the spider and inspected it nervously with its curled antennae. Suddenly it grabbed the spider's leg with its mandibles and began to drag it away with surprising speed across the open ground.

And not a moment too soon, because just as the wasp and spider cleared the roadway a thundering herd of about forty young kayakers and their river guides trammeled over the site where I had spent the past three-quarters of an hour on wasp watch. I paid them little attention as I crouched and crabbed along the access road paralleling the railroad tracks, following the wasp's progress through my lens.

Every now and again the wasp would abandon the spider, apparently wandering off to reconnoiter the next leg of her journey. After a few minutes, I could see the wasp negotiating its way back through the tangled growth. As before, the wasp briefly inspected the spider with its antennae before grabbing a leg with its mouth and setting off on a new course.

The sunlight was beginning to fade when the spider wasp ditched her booty once again. I had two more shots left and decided to wait for the wasp to return one more time. I waited another ten minutes or so for the wasp to come back, but it never did. I decided to call it a day and could only assume that the wasp was out somewhere, simultaneously excavating a spider's grave and preparing a wasp's nursery.

Carpenter Bees
Lead Boring Lives

The warm spring air is filled with the comings and goings of large, noisy blue black carpenter bees as they patrol dead limbs and wooden structures in search of mates and nesting sites. Like all ants, bees, and wasps, only female carpenter bees can sting, but they are relatively docile creatures. The more aggressive males are readily distinguished by their white faces and are incapable of stinging at all. Nevertheless, the "in-your-face" aerial tactics of the males, stingless or not, can be quite intimidating when you unwittingly stumble into their territory.

Large carpenter bees are all placed in the aptly named genus *Xylocopa*, or "wood cutter." Most of the seven hundred–plus species of *Xylocopa* known worldwide live in the tropics. Of the seven species living in the United States, only two are found in the East, both of which occur in Virginia. The eastern carpenter bee, *X. virginica*, is known throughout the state, while the southern carpenter bee, *X. micans*, lives in the southeastern part of the commonwealth. Unlike the social honeybee imported from Europe, the solitary eastern and southern carpenter bees are both native to North America.

The relatively large head of the carpenter bee is as wide as its bristly thorax, or midsection, and houses the muscles that drive the powerful wood-chewing mandibles. The body is about 1.5 inches long and generally resembles a bumblebee. However, its black or metallic blue black abdomen lacks the bumblebee's brightly colored patches of hair.

The spring generation of adult carpenter bees matures the previous summer, flies about briefly, and then retires back inside the nest chamber or some other protected place to spend the winter. At the first signs of spring, carpenter bees emerge from their hiding places to search for food and mates. Males become quite territorial, claiming for their own landmarks such as prominent plants, bare patches of soil, and walls up to sixty feet away from nesting sites. They aggressively drive off other males and females moving through their territory, as well as other flying insects. The size and location of each male's territory often changes from day to day.

Many male carpenter bees patrol patches of flowers and will attempt to mate with females gathering pollen and nectar. Courtship occurs with much buzzing and aerial acrobatics, with the pair flying apart and coming back together several times. Mating takes place primarily in the spring and, to a lesser degree, in the fall.

Female eastern carpenter bees build their nests in dead trees or logs, or in unfinished wooden structures. They prefer nesting sites with southern or eastern exposures and may chew their tunnels anywhere from one to thirty feet off the ground. Females excavate the future homes of their offspring nonstop, working throughout the night and over several days with powerful jaws; their incessant chewing is sometimes audible from several feet away. Sawdust is pushed out of the nest with the head, legs, and abdomen merely to clear a path down the tunnel. Unlike termites, they don't use the wood as food, but instead rely on pollen and nectar for nourishment.

The nest consists of a single round entrance the same diameter as the bee—about ½ inch wide. The entrance burrow is short, roughly the body length of the bee. Once the entrance burrow is complete, the female soon turns left or right at a 90-degree angle to follow the grain of the timber. She then chews two or more parallel tunnels, each up to fourteen inches long. The grain of the wood determines the direction of the tunnels, which are slightly wider in diameter than the entrance hole.

At the completion of the tunnel-building activities in May or June, a female carpenter bee begins to lay her eggs. She lays her first egg at the blind end of the tunnel on a doughy pill made up of pollen and about the thickness of a kidney bean. The pollen provided by the female will be the only food available to the developing bee larvae. The surrounding wood is chewed into a yellowish pulp to form a disklike partition between each of the six to eight eggs laid in the tunnel. After the brood has developed, matured, chewed their way through the partitions, and left the nest, the old nests are sometimes recycled, either as nesting or overwintering sites. New occupants thoroughly renovate the site to remove dirt, old cocoons, and waste left by the previous tenants, including other bees, wasps, and their parasites.

Flowers provide the sole source of food and most of the water for carpenter bees. To maximize their foraging time for pollen and nectar, carpenter bees mark the flowers they visit with a repellant chemical, or pheromone. By marking flowers they can effectively skip blossoms whose nectar and pollen stores have been recently depleted by other carpenter bees. The repellant pheromone remains effective for up to ten minutes at a time.

Baltimore orioles eat adult bees while northern flickers and red-bellied woodpeckers chop into the nests in search of plump larvae. Ants invade carpenter bee nests not only to attack and eat the helpless larvae but also to raid their food stores. At least two species of bee flies parasitize the larvae of eastern carpenter bees by laying their eggs just inside the tunnel entrance. The maggots hatch and attack the developing bee larvae.

In spite of this seemingly endless parade of predators and parasitoids, the greatest enemies of carpenter bees are humans. They destroy the nests of carpenter bees, as well as their nesting sites, by land clearing and construction projects. Left without their usual nesting sites, carpenter bees are forced to build their nests in the unfinished timbers of buildings and other wooden structures.

Male bees may be an annoyance if their territories are too close to human activities, but remember, they cannot sting. Nesting females are relatively docile, but will chew tunnels in exposed rafters and framework of old houses, picnic tables, rail fences, posts, trellises, and other unfinished wood surfaces. Left in their wake are piles of yellow sawdust and small splashes of yellowish excrement that accumulates into unsightly stains. Woodpeckers attracted to the nests in search of food may further damage wooden structures.

Carpenter bees rarely attack painted or varnished wood. If there is a problem with carpenter bees, simply apply a coat of paint to the wood. Plugging nest entrances is most effective when all bees are removed from the tunnels and unfinished surfaces are painted. Always consult a licensed pest-control operator or carefully read application instructions on commercially available insecticides before using chemicals of any kind to control unwanted insects.

Tolerance is the key. The truth is that the damage caused by carpenter bees to wooden structures is seldom severe and is easily offset by their pollination services. All of us are absolutely dependent upon the link between pollinators and plants. As we alter and modify the natural environment, we displace not only individual species but also the relationships that exist between them. Nowhere is this disruption more evident than with the phenomenon of pollination, considered by some conservationists to be a "threatened ecological service." Our gardens, fields, orchards, and forests would not be nearly as lush or productive were it not for the tireless efforts of insect pollinators such as the carpenter bee. Besides, whether they are visiting flowers or engaged in nest building, carpenter bees are just darned fascinating animals to watch!

The Buzz on Bumblebees

I recently happened across a bumblebee snuggled among the petals of a flower. The listless black and yellow fuzzball was covered with dew and had apparently spent the night out in the field. But as the sun burned off the early-morning mist, she quickly came to life and resumed her rounds among the flowers. Soon dozens of bumblebees were in view, all diligently collecting pollen and nectar for their colonies. Their relatively short wings seemed wholly inadequate for propelling their chunky bodies, laden with both pollen and nectar, through the air.

More than three hundred species of bumblebees are known, mostly from Asia. Unlike honeybees, all forty-one species of bumblebees living in North America are native to the continent. Although some species are festively clothed in white, orange, or red, Virginia's eight species are all dressed in the more familiar black and yellow. Their large, bulky bodies resemble those of carpenter, digger, and mining bees. However, the relatively small head and hairy abdomens serve to distinguish bumblebees from their cousins. Like honeybees, pollen baskets adorn the back legs of the queens and workers of seven of our Virginia bumblebee species. No other bees have these baskets.

Bumblebees are among the few insects that can control their body temperature. In cold weather, queens and workers vibrate their wing muscles to warm themselves, allowing them to continue flying and foraging, while lower temperatures immobilize most other insects. Their bulky, hairy bodies help to conserve warmth and energy. As a result, bumblebees are found above the Arctic Circle and in high-elevation habitats.

As with all ants, bees, and wasps, only female bumblebees are capable of stinging, but they do so only to defend themselves and their nest. Predators quickly learn to avoid these hairy and brightly marked animals. As a result, several species of beetles and flies sport bumblebee colors to fool birds and other predators. American burying beetles are hairless, but their black and yellow colors look very bumblebeelike when they take to the air. Some robber flies not only copy the colors of bumblebees, but also mimic their hairy bodies.

Bumblebees are social insects living in colonies led by a queen and populated with up to 150 sterile female workers. The nest is underground, usually in a preexisting hollow underneath an old tree stump or in an abandoned rodent nest. They are sensitive to habitat degradation and are seldom found in lands cleared for agricultural, industrial, and residential purposes.

The larvae develop on the chamber floor in wax cells resembling pots and are cared for by other workers and fed a steady diet of pollen and nectar. Warm-bodied queens, workers, and drones all pitch in to incubate the brood. Small amounts of honey and pollen are also stored as food in potlike wax cells, but these are kept separate from the brood. The internal architecture of the nest is not organized into neat layers of combs as with honeybees. Instead, new cells are built on top of older ones, resulting in a continually growing, moundlike mass.

With the approach of autumn, each colony begins producing reproductives—queens and drones. Queens lay unfertilized eggs that develop into drones, while fertilized eggs become future queens. Once mature, the reproductives leave the nest to mate with new queens and drones from other colonies. By winter, the queen, drones, and workers have all died off, leaving only the newly mated queens hibernating in the soil.

Bumblebees are important pollinators of many native herbaceous plants and woody shrubs. Their large bodies and long tongues determine which flowers they will visit. They are especially well suited for pollinating snapdragons and other deep throated flowers. They have long been used commercially to pollinate crops such as eggplants, melons, and wild blueberries. Bumblebees are also effective in orchards, pollinating almonds, apples, and cherries. Researchers have manipulated bumblebee queen behavior so they skip hibernation and produce colonies year-round, making them available to pollinate more kinds of crops. They are now considered essential for pollinating greenhouse crops of strawberries, peppers, and tomatoes.

To see a photographic checklist and identify Virginia bumblebees, visit http://pick4.pick.uga.edu/mp/20q?guide=Bumblebees.

The Giant Hornet,
a Wasp's Wasp

While roaming about Pocahontas State Park just before Labor Day, I heard the shrill cry of a cicada. It wasn't the usual amorous mating call, but one of pure distress. I turned around and looked upward, expecting to see a blue jay or some other bird brandishing a bulky insect in its beak. But instead I saw a cicada, firmly held in the grasp of a wasp, plunging toward the open patch of ground at my feet. At last, I had my chance to photograph a cicada killer grappling with its prey. I raced to my car, hurriedly assembled my camera, and, when I returned, found the cicada still in the wasp's death grip.

Lying on my belly, I crawled over to the battling pair and composed the photograph. The wasp darted away as the flash went off, leaving the mortally wounded cicada behind. But soon the wasp returned to the scene and began circling its victim. I backed away to give the wasp the opportunity to reclaim her hard-won prey.

Using powerful jaws, she quickly began to rip chunks of flesh from the cicada's soft underbelly, its legs still twitching. This behavior seemed odd to me. Cicada killers typically haul off their victims in one piece, not piecemeal. Watching the scene through my camera lens, I soon recognized that the wasp was not a solitary cicada killer but a social European import, the giant hornet. An eastern yellow jacket soon appeared on the scene. The yellow jacket, an American cousin of the hornet, was hovering around the periphery like a jackal, waiting for its turn to scavenge the remains of the cicada's body.

I had encountered giant hornets earlier in the year. With snow still on the ground, most insects had long retired to their protected hideaways, such as beneath stones and under loose bark. I found a large dead oak with its bark already peeling away. The soft, punky wood offered refuge to numerous adult spiders, bugs, beetles, and their immature stages, all in a state of suspended animation. As I carefully poked through the remains of the once-mighty tree, I came across the largest hornet I had ever seen. Its prominent reddish brown head immediately identified this individual as a giant hornet, probably an overwintering queen.

By sequestering themselves each winter in a variety of nooks and crannies—including downed logs—those queens that survive the killing frosts serve as the nucleus for new giant hornet colonies in the spring. Each of these queens begins construction on a new nest, but it is left up to the succeeding generations of workers to finish the job. Unlike bees, giant hornets do not use wax to build their nests. Instead, they use their powerful jaws to scrape wood from trees and fences. Mixed with saliva, the pulpy concoction dries into sheets of coarse, brittle paper that are pressed into the makings of a nest. The completed nest resembles a misshapen ball of papier-mâché. Inside are five or six horizontally stacked layers of brood cells. Each layer is separated by the approximate height of the hornet and attached to one another by a centrally placed column of paper. Each layer of brood cells resembles a honeycomb and measures approximately eight inches across. There may be as many as 1,500 brood cells in a single nest.

Nests are typically built in hollow trees, under porches, beneath roof overhangs, and in basements. Exposed, suspended nests are enveloped in a brownish gray paper covering, while more protected nests, such as those in tree hollows, may lack this covering. Completed nests vary from 2 to 3 feet in length and 10 to 20 inches in diameter. A single nest may contain hundreds of wasps. In one late-season nest, an entomologist in North Carolina recovered 29 queens, 142 workers, 116 males, 95 pupae, and 31 larvae.

Giant hornets were first described in Europe over two hundred years ago by Carl von Linné, or Carolus Linnaeus, as he is often known. He was a Swedish naturalist and architect of the system by which today's scientists name living and prehistoric organisms. He christened this impressive wasp *Vespa crabro*. Its name is derived from two Latin words, both meaning wasp. The large and powerful hornet, ever-present during the summer and early fall, must have seemed like the wasp of all wasps. Queen hornets reach nearly 1½ inches in length, while the sterile female workers and males are somewhat smaller.

The exact date of this large, showy insect's introduction into North America is not known. Giant hornets were first observed in New York State around 1840. The earliest specimens found in museum collections were captured in 1854. By 1931, giant hornets were well established in the northeastern United States. It was reported in Fredericksburg, Virginia, in 1939 and Raleigh, North Carolina, in 1941. Today, giant hornets are known to occur as far north as the province of Quebec, south to Georgia, and west to Indiana. Over time, these large and powerful insects will no doubt populate virtually all of eastern North America.

Giant hornets are not particularly aggressive, rarely stinging for any other reason than in defense of their nest. Like many wasps, the adults eat other insects and drink nectar and sap from various plants. In Europe, flies may constitute up to 90 percent of the giant hornet's diet. They will also attack other wasps, bees, and beetles. Larger insects, such as dragonflies and cicadas, are also consumed. Giant hornets are reported to occasionally damage plants by girdling small branches and chewing holes in larger branches, either in an effort to gather materials to manufacture paper for nest building or to collect sap. They are also known to feed upon ripening fruit. Their plump carnivorous larvae, which live suspended upside down in the hexagonal brood cells of the nest, are fed a steady diet of masticated insects until they pupate.

In fall, workers are still busily collecting pollen and nectar from goldenrod and other flowers, but their days are numbered. Cool fall temperatures mark the end the road for the female workers, males, and old queens. The bodies of dead and dying wasps can be found strewn about the ground in parks and woodlands where giant hornets are common. Soon entire colonies of giant hornets will be dead, save for the new crop of young, fertilized queens who have tucked themselves away for the winter. It is their mission to see that the population of North American giant hornets survive and thrive for yet another season.

The Paper Trail
Starts Here

We take paper for granted, using it for newspapers, magazines, books, utensils, and packaging of all sorts. Yet, before the first human paper makers began developing their craft, insect artisans such as paper wasps of the cosmopolitan genus *Polistes* had been making their own paper for hundreds of thousands, perhaps millions of years. *Polistes* comes to us from the Greek word meaning "founder of the city." This is no doubt in reference to the fact that paper wasps live in colonies of related individuals who share the tasks of nest building, brood care, food gathering, and defense. Their paper is wrought from a pulpy mixture of water, saliva, and plant fibers scraped from posts, fences, dead limbs, stems, or dried grasses. The material is so tough that it was once the preferred material used for wadding in muzzle-loading guns.

Paper wasps are long and slender insects reaching nearly ¾ of an inch in length. At rest, their four smoky wings fold lengthwise over a spindle-shaped abdomen. Their black or rusty red bodies are often marked with orange or yellow bands. In the New World, dozens of paper wasp species are found from southern Canada to South America. Like their relatives the hornets and yellow jackets, paper wasps construct nests of tough gray or brown paper called carton. Unlike the enclosed and multitiered nests of hornets and yellow jackets, paper wasp nests are exposed, consisting of a single, circular layer of hexagonal cells.

Temperate North American paper wasps have annual life cycles. Beginning in spring, fertilized queens leave their protected winter hideaways to begin new colonies. Their nests seem to pop up overnight in sheltered spots under tree branches, around homes and sheds, or some other overhang. Laboring day and night, the queen fashions her paper nest one cell at a time. The cells open downward and are primarily used for housing brood. When the larvae are mature and ready to pupate, the adults cap the cells with more paper. By late summer, a mature nest can have as many as two hundred cells and support up to fifty adult wasps. The banded color pattern of each nest reveals the variety of sources of plant fibers used in the nest's construction.

The first cluster of cells is thumb-sized and suspended by a slender stalk strong enough to support the burgeoning nest and all of its future inhabitants. The sole point of contact to a solid surface, the stalk functions as the nest's first line of defense. The wasps can easily defend this narrow bridge from ants and other crawling marauders intent on stealing eggs and larvae.

A single queen usually initiates nest construction. By the time the first brood of sterile workers has emerged, two to six subordinate queens may have joined her on the nest. Like other animals, paper wasps develop dominance hierarchies, or pecking orders. A dominant female demands and receives the greatest amounts of food, lays more eggs, and performs fewer physical tasks, such as nest building and food gathering, than the subordinate queens. She also eats or destroys eggs laid in cells by the other queens. The dominant queen reinforces the nest hierarchy by frequent aggressive encounters ranging from simple posturing to leg biting and grappling. The queen at the top of the pecking order has fully developed ovaries, while her subordinates have progressively smaller reproductive organs. Within a day or two the aggression subsides as the subordinates begin to settle into their respective roles.

The dominant queen lays a single egg in each cell. The eggs hatch and develop into plump, carnivorous larvae and are fed a steady diet of pellets consisting of chewed-up insects and spiders. Wasps acting as nursemaids are rewarded for their efforts by the larvae, which offer up a deliciously sweet fluid secreted by their salivary glands.

Development from egg to adult is rapid, taking about forty-eight days on average. Roughly three widely overlapping broods are produced each season. The first generation of larvae develops into sterile female workers. The queen continues to start new cells and lay eggs, but now the workers finish the cells and feed the larvae. As many as two hundred individuals may be raised annually, but mortality is high, and only twenty to thirty individuals are usually found in the nest at any given time.

In fall, the queen lays fertilized and unfertilized eggs that will develop into future queens and males, respectively. Soon the shorter-lived worker population is almost entirely replaced by the reproductive castes. Eventually the queen, nearing the end of her life, stops laying eggs, and the colony soon goes into decline. The short-lived males eventually abandon the nests and are soon followed by the future queens. Mating takes place on nearby sunlit areas or in cavities destined to be overwintering sites for the soon-to-be-fertilized queens. The males die off as the days become cooler and shorter, leaving the mated females to endure the chill of winter alone.

Paper wasps are considered beneficial predators by informed gardeners who tolerate their presence. Flying wasps meander around shrubs and other vegetation as they search for insects and spiders to feed their larvae. Rather than using their sting, they use powerful mandibles to kill their prey. Adult wasps consume pollen and nectar for their own nourishment.

Paper wasps are not particularly aggressive, and removal of their nests is not always warranted. Simply approaching a nest closely is not necessarily viewed as an attack by the wasps. However, they are quite capable of aggressively defending their nest with a barrage of extremely painful stings. Unlike the barbed sting of a honeybee that remains in the flesh of the victim, the smooth stinger of the paper wasp allows it to sting repeatedly at will. Male paper wasps are incapable of stinging, as are the males of all ants, bees, and wasps. But, unless you are good at distinguishing paper wasp genders, it's best to treat them all as females!

Mudslingers and Spider Killers

The most familiar of wasps, such as hornets, yellow jackets, and paper wasps, are decidedly social creatures, living in cooperative groups that build paper nests and feed the young. However, the vast majority of wasps are solitary creatures, a few of which are known as mud daubers. These loners construct mud nests on various surfaces protected from weather and direct sun including trees, rocks, posts, and walls. A typical nest usually consists of several chambers partitioned by mud walls, each packed with living, yet paralyzed, spiders immobilized by the female mud dauber's sting. These provisions will serve as food for the single wasp larva developing in each chamber. Adult mud daubers are not so carnivorous, preferring instead to dine on nectar and pollen.

Some nests are finely crafted, resembling pipe organs and narrow-necked pots upon completion, while others look more like a hurled clod of mud. Hundreds of trips to a nearby mud puddle are required to build just one nest. A few species do not make nests of their own at all, relying instead on the previous labors of other mud daubers. Only females build nests and gather food; males do not participate in these tasks at all. Nest building and egg laying take place in the late summer and fall, after which the female soon dies. Larval development proceeds rapidly. The mature larvae are pale yellowish and do not quite reach an inch in length. They pass the winter wrapped in a thin, brown, papery cocoon inside the chamber. Pupation finally takes place in spring, and the adult emerges soon thereafter.

The black-and-yellow mud dauber, *Sceliphron caementarium,* is about an inch long and resembles a paper wasp. However, its short abdomen, which is attached by a long and slender waist, is predominately black instead of yellow. They are found throughout the United States and southern Canada and are frequently seen around puddles rolling up small balls of mud to carry back to nest-building sites. Their clodlike mud nest houses from two to six elongate and parallel chambers, each laid side by side. Although they will use various spider species, female black-and-yellow mud daubers have a decided preference for orb weavers, followed by crab spiders and jumping spiders. They carefully pack the spiders into each cell, using their heads as battering rams.

The iridescent blue mud dauber, *Chalybion californicum,* is also widespread. Instead of building a nest of its own, it relies on the labors of the black-and-yellow mud dauber. Using water to open the outer, sealed chambers, a blue mud dauber dumps out the contents and then packs it with her own spiders, mostly black widows. She lays a single egg, seals the chamber, and leaves.

The organ pipe mud dauber, *Trypoxylon politum*, is all black and ranges in length from ½ to ¾ of an inch. This species is common throughout the East and constructs conspicuous nests of long, parallel tubes on exposed walls and other flat surfaces. Each tube is constructed with mud of one or more colors collected from different sites and takes anywhere from three hours to all day to construct. Tubes vary in length and contain as many as eight cells when completed. Old tubes are often reused, repaired, and extended. Male pipe organ mud daubers will stand guard while the female is away foraging almost exclusively for orb weavers and collecting mud.

Mud dauber nests are sealed microcosms that demonstrate a fascinating array of ecological relationships. Nests collected in fall and winter are free of adult mud daubers and make great classroom investigations. They contain not only immature wasps and their spider food but also a variety of insect scavengers, wasp and fly parasites, and other predators. Female mud daubers are seldom aggressive and sting only when handled. Unfortunately, some fail to appreciate these architectural dynamos and their choice of nest-building sites and needlessly persecute them as a nuisance.

To obtain information about using mud dauber nests in the classroom and other educational activities with insects, visit http://www.wowbugs.com/teaching/teaching.html.

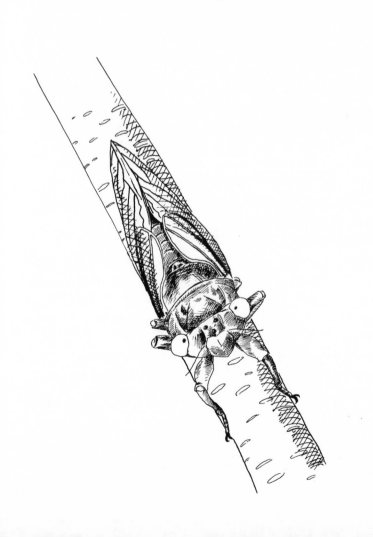

6

Bugs, Spiders,
and Other
Musings

Since moving to Virginia, I have felt like a kid in a candy store. Whenever I go out into the woods and wetlands with my camera, I am always rewarded with seeing new and challenging subject matter to capture on film. Although beetles are my primary reason for getting out and about, other insects and spiders often capture my attention. In 2003, there was a massive periodical cicada emergence (Brood IX) that propelled me on a three-hour drive to western Virginia. Whenever I look back on that trip and the images I captured of them with their bulging red eyes, it is as if I have entered a time machine that instantly transports me back to that hot and muggy afternoon in Patrick County. I also went through a period when I wanted to find harvestmen, those leggy arachnids similar to spiders. My goal was to shoot as many species as possible and to capture their interesting behaviors on film.

Even organisms that are neither plants nor animals sometimes catch my eye. I have long noticed the subtle or fluorescent colors, crusty or leafy textures, and rosettelike patterns of lichens plastered on rocks, tree trunks, and limbs—even some buildings and other structures. These seemingly alien combinations of fungi and cyanobacteria living as one among Virginia's exposed rocky outcrops or shady woods are always a pleasure to shoot because they never run or fly away.

My searches for these six-legged animals and their relatives have long helped me to keep in touch with the rich diversity of all organisms as they struggle to survive in their own place and season. Each of these species has its own history and story to tell and could easily provide a lifetime's worth of observation, study, and photography. It is this realization that reminds me that life is all too short and that we owe it to ourselves to see and do as much as we possibly can before it is too late.

Scratching That
17-Year Itch

Where were you in 1987? I was chasing beetles and my doctoral degree in entomology in South Africa. Ronald Reagan was in the White House. *Three Men and a Baby* was tops at the box office. Halley's Comet had many of us squinting up into the starry night. Gas was only $1.15 a gallon. And it was also the last year that periodical cicadas of Brood X saw the sun. That is, until 2004.

That was the year that all of the adults of Brood X emerged within days or weeks of one another from May through early June. They will not be seen again, save for a few possible stragglers, until 2031. By early June 2004, millions of these large, red-eyed insects emerged across parts of northern and western Virginia, as well as in fourteen other states across the eastern United States.

Population densities ranged from 30,000 to 3.5 million individuals per hectare in some areas. This massive emergence overwhelms predators and guarantees that most cicadas will survive to reproduce. It is also guaranteed to unnecessarily alarm people. Unfortunately, their large size and clumsy behavior needlessly inspire fear in many people. Rest assured that all cicadas are incapable of biting or stinging. And while the collective throbbing wail of the males calling the silent females is a great annoyance to many, fortunately for the annoyed among us, male cicadas stop calling at dusk.

Since 1987, the subterranean offspring of Brood X labored in total darkness, burrowing as deep as twenty inches beneath the surface to suck a cocktail of water, amino acids, and minerals from tree roots. The annual flowering cycle of these trees, as reflected by seasonal chemical changes in their sap, may help the young cicadas keep track of time and season.

The sap-feeding activities of the cicada larvae are of little consequence to healthy trees. However, the massive emergence of adults does cause some damage to twigs of young trees and nursery stock. The adults do not feed, but the females will split open twigs in order to lay their eggs inside. The twigs eventually break off and fall to the ground where the larvae hatch and dig into the soil.

Every thirteen or seventeen years, the larvae of periodical cicadas must shift their biological imperatives from feeding and growing to mating and reproduction. Starting in April, the larvae begin making tentative preparations for their relatively brief four- to six-week frolic in the sun. Dime-sized holes appear under trees, some with mud turrets. For a few weeks, when moisture and temperature conditions are just right, millions of larvae leave their burrows forever under the cover of night and crawl up the nearest tree, house, or fence.

Gripping the surface firmly with their claws, the larva's back soon splits open to reveal a new animal with a soft, pale, plump body and crumpled wings. Within thirty minutes, the wings of the newly emerged periodical cicada are fully formed, though still soft and pliable. By morning, the cicada's body will be sturdy enough for the rigors of flight.

The most familiar element of this amazing late-night transformation remains behind for all to see—the shed exoskeleton, or exuviae. The exuviae (both singular and plural) is the hollowed-out husk, or skin, of the larva and is complete down to the smallest detail. The exuviae clearly reveals the larva's oversized, reinforced forelegs designed for a life of digging underground and the short, sucking mouthparts for piercing roots and sucking up fluids.

Most cicadas emerge annually, so we see and hear them every year. But the appearance of periodical cicadas is a relatively infrequent event. It is strictly a North American phenomenon and was noted as early as 1666. Since then, seven species of periodical cicadas have been discovered; three that emerge every seventeen years and four that emerge every thirteen years. Species with both cycles occur in Virginia.

Populations of cicadas with 13- or 17-year life cycles within specific geographic ranges are called broods. Each brood emerges in different years and often contains more than one species of periodic cicada. In 1898, a system was devised for tracking the emergence of periodical cicadas by assigning a Roman numeral to each brood. Broods of 17-year cicadas were designated I–XVII, while 13-year cicadas are identified by XVIII–XXIII. The brood that emerged in 1893 was arbitrarily called Brood I. Since the turn of the twentieth century, several broods of periodical cicadas have become extinct, victims of logging, forest fires, urbanization, or deforestation caused by the ravages of the gypsy moth.

Brood X was first documented in 1715 and is currently receiving considerable media attention because its broad range cuts across several major metropolitan areas. Broods I, II, V, IX, XIV, and XIX also occur in Virginia. The next major emergence of periodical cicadas in the commonwealth is Brood II and will occur throughout most of Piedmont region in 2013.

I cut my teeth on Brood IX. I had never seen periodical cicadas before when I learned in June 2003 that their emergence was in full swing in Patrick County. I packed up my camera and drove west for nearly four hours until I reached Philpott Reservoir.

I was completely unprepared for the spectacle before me. Cicadas were everywhere, flying, crawling, calling, and egg-laying. Their exuviae clung to the shrubbery like Christmas ornaments or were strewn about on the ground like confetti. I had the luxury of going home to relative peace and quiet at the end of the day; I cannot imagine what it must be like to be surrounded by these raucous animals day after day for a month or more.

Still, my experience that day was no less awe-inspiring than when I walked among trees quietly festooned with overwintering monarch butterflies in Mexico, or when I was surrounded by thundering herds of wildebeest on their annual migration across the Mara River in Kenya. Seeing these ancient and cyclical events reminds me that we are not stewards of the natural world, but a part of it.

To see the distribution of periodical cicadas in Virginia by county and their years of emergence, visit http://www.ext.vt.edu/pubs/entomology/444-276/444-276.html.

Check out the calls and years of emergence of periodical ci-

cadas, plus other cicada links, at http://insects.ummz.lsa.umich
.edu/fauna/michigan-cicadas.

And Along
Came a Spider

True confession: I am a recovering arachnophobe. Long fascinated by insects, my exuberance may quickly turn to unease when it
comes to spiders. Yet, to my knowledge, none has ever caused me
harm in any way. With this fact in mind, I decided to deal with my
irrational, yet common anxiety head-on by immersing myself in
spider books, articles and . . . live spiders. While director of the
Insect Zoo at the Natural History Museum of Los Angeles, I cared
for a collection of fifty large, hairy tarantulas and other arachnids
for several years, an endeavor that went a long way toward helping
me to conquer my creeps. As a result, I became hooked on these
amazing animals.

Roughly 36,000 of the world's animals are spiders. The spider
fore body, or cephalothorax, bears up to eight eyes, fangs, and
eight legs. The fangs move up and down in a stabbing motion or
swing from side to side like ice tongs. Spiders depend on their
hollow fangs to inject venom laced with digestive enzymes that
simultaneously disables and liquefies small animal prey. Leglike
pedipalps found on either side of the fangs are used like fingers to
help manipulate prey. Males use special organs on the tips of their
pedipalps for storing sperm until they can find a mate.

Silk is the hallmark of spiders, and they use it for many purposes.
Spider silk is a protein produced in liquid form by special abdominal
glands. A battery of spigots mounted on three pairs of abdominal
spinnerets on the abdomen forms a complicated pump-and-valve
pressure system that changes the liquid into dry fibers of silk. Spiders can manipulate the thickness, strength, and stretchiness of
their silk. Ounce for ounce stronger than steel, black widow silk
was used as the cross hairs in gun sights during World War II.

Although most spiders are harmless, there are two American
species that manage to attract a great deal of attention: black wid-

ows and recluse spiders. Black widows spin their webs in closets, attics, basements, stumps, under rocks, and in abandoned rodent burrows. Two species are known from Virginia—the northern widow, *L. variolus*, and southern widow, *L. mactans.* The glossy black females of both species have distinct red hourglasses splashed on their bellies. The much smaller males are tan and variably marked with white. Sometimes after mating, an exhausted male attempts to leave the web only to be mistaken as food by its hungry mate.

The bite of these widows causes tenderness at the site of the wound, severe muscular pain and stiffness, sweating, and vomiting. Fortunately, they are not aggressive and their bites are easily avoided and seldom fatal. In the unlikely event of a bite, place a bag of ice on the wound, keep calm, and seek medical treatment immediately.

The brown recluse, *Loxosceles reclusa,* is a leggy, medium-sized, brown spider. Known as "violin spiders" due a fiddle-shaped marking on their cephalothorax, recluse spiders are naturally abundant in the Mississippi River drainage. They do not occur in Virginia, except for the occasional accidental introduction of an individual spider. Recluse spiders sometimes become established in buildings and barns where there is ample insect food, but prefer instead to live under stones or in caves. Unlike that of black widows, brown recluse venom acts locally. The bite wound turns purplish and then black, is slow to heal, and may scar badly. A similar species, the Mediterranean recluse, *L. rufescens,* may also turn up in Virginia as a vagrant.

My wife, Paula, is also fascinated with arachnids, which is fortunate not only for me but also for the numerous spiders that inevitably wander through our home. She carefully coaxes these eight-legged interlopers into a container, examines them briefly, and then releases them outside.

Residing in the messy cobwebs among the dark recesses of our basement are slender-bodied spiders with impossibly long, thin legs. This yellowish gray spider is called the European cellar spider, *Pholcus phalangioides,* and is established throughout North America, Australia, and New Zealand. It is sometimes confused with another arachnid that never builds a web, the daddy longlegs, or harvestman. With just a single body region and segmented abdomen, the harvestman is not a true spider at all.

Other spiders are less settled in their ways and are usually encountered as they are simply passing through. For example, while I was working at the dining room table, my attention was drawn to a bulky male jumping spider, *Phidippus audax.* Commonly known as the bold jumper, this audacious arachnid eyed me with caution as it flashed its iridescent green fang bases in my direction while waving its bristly, flaglike pedipalps in the air. The two large forward-looking eyes are shaped like a couple of test tubes and take up more room inside its head than its brain. By contracting powerful muscles in the abdomen, this handsome jumping spider forces body fluid into its hind legs to launch itself into the air. Some jumping spiders can propel themselves forty times their body length!

Brownish funnelweb spiders occupy silken retreats in our lawn, on shrubbery, or draped across the corners of our windows. Their hunting grounds are limited to the thick, multilayered sheet of silk surrounding their funnel-shaped lair. When a small insect hits the sheet, the spider rushes out in a blur of activity and drags its victim back to the safety of its retreat to dine.

The bright apple green body of the lynx spider, *Peucetia viridans,* is perfectly camouflaged against the flush of summer growth in fields and along roadsides. Using stealth instead of silk, it pounces on its prey with long yellow legs sprinkled with black spines.

Another group of web-free hunters is the fishing spiders of the genus *Dolomedes.* Four species of these robust and conspicuous arachnids live along the edges of Virginia's permanent ponds, streams, and rivers. They use the water's surface tension as their web, attacking live insects trapped on the surface. Fishing spiders occasionally dive beneath the surface to escape their enemies— such as spider wasps—and to capture minnows.

One of the larger Virginia spiders is seldom seen, preferring instead a life underground. Male trap door spiders, *Ummidia,* are often mistaken for young, shiny tarantulas as they wander about at night in search of the much larger female. Young male and female trap-doors dig smooth, straight burrows with spiny rakes on their fangs. Lined with velvety silk, their burrows are concealed by hinged lids of papery silk woven with bits of debris.

In fall, hidden among the spikes of goldenrod, the crab spider, *Misumena vatia*, lies in wait. Like crabs, they have the ability to move sideways or backwards with equal speed and agility. Their first two pairs of legs are long and thick for grabbing flower-visiting bees, beetles, butterflies, flies, and wasps. This crab spider, along with a few other related species, has the limited ability to change colors to match its background. It is not unusual to find pink, yellow, or white *Misumena* spiders.

From time to time, my discomfort with spiders resurfaces, especially when a dark leggy one zips by unexpectedly. Certainly these small creatures are more terrified of me. I take a moment to remind myself that they are the primary predators of many insect pests and seldom cause any bodily harm. And when I think of their staggering array of forms and behaviors and what great photographic subjects they make, my apprehension once again turns to admiration.

Check out the Spider Room at the Mathematics and Science Center in Mechanicsville at http://www.spiderroom.info.

For Doodlebugs,
Life is the Pits

During the warmer parts of the years, you can find the dimpled hunting grounds of a special group of antlion larvae, fondly known as doodlebugs. These odd little creatures construct their conical sand pits on sandy patches strewn along streams and rivers. Occasionally they will take up residence in the undisturbed corners of sandboxes and playgrounds. Whether in the wild or in developed habitats, the pits of doodlebugs usually appear underneath the edges of shrubbery or at the foot of rocky overhangs and walls.

In spite of their cute name, doodlebugs are fierce, opportunistic predators, eating anything they can catch. The larvae of other species of antlions are free-ranging predators that ambush small insect prey on the branched pathways winding through trees and shrubs, or among the labyrinth of nooks and crannies in leaf litter. But doodlebugs are decidedly sedentary; they stake their entire fortunes on sandy pitfall traps to catch their food.

Doodlebugs spend their winters deep in sand, just beyond the reach of killing frosts. But, with the arrival of spring, they ascend to the surface. They always push through the sand backwards, using their pudgy, bristly, and wedge-shaped bodies as plows. These busy insects seem to wander about aimlessly as they search for just the right location, leaving winding furrows, or doodles, in their wake.

Once they settle into a spot, doodlebugs begin spiraling downward, using their flat heads like shovels to flip loose sand out of the developing pit. Around and around they go, in ever tighter and deeper circles, until they have excavated an inverted, cone-shaped trap. The slippery sides of the trap have a steep pitch. Once the trap is completed, the doodlebug quietly lies buried in wait, with only the sharp tips of its scythelike mandibles poking out of the sand to give away its location.

When an ant or similar small and hapless animal stumbles into the pit, the doodlebug snaps into action. By violently flicking its shovel-like head from the bottom of the pit, the hungry larva simultaneously pelts its intended victim with sand and pulls the rug out from under its feet. Unable to gain purchase on the continually shifting sands, the struggling prey soon tires and slides down to the bottom of the pit, its fate sealed.

Like all insects with chewing mouthparts, doodlebugs have two sets of jaws. But theirs are modified and lock together to form a pair of hollow tubes that serve as both syringes and straws. When the jaws snap shut on prey, they become a delivery system for injecting a cocktail of digestive fluids. These enzymes soon turn the internal organs and tissues into soup. Once its prey has been liquefied, the doodlebug sucks the guts out through its strawlike jaws, leaving only a dried, shriveled husk of exoskeleton behind.

Doodlebugs and the larvae of antlion relatives are unique among insects in that their digestive tracts are not yet fully developed. As a result, their waste products are stored for up to three years, and are only voided from their bodies when they emerge from the pupa as an adult. Doodlebugs pupate inside a cocoon spun from silk produced by kidneylike organs called Malpighian tubules.

Adult antlions typically emerge in summer. They have long, slender bodies and resemble flimsy grayish damselflies. Their spiny legs are used to capture insect prey on the wing, just like damselflies. Unlike damselflies, the antennae of antlions are relatively long and thick. The four wings are translucent and lacey, supported by an intricate network of fine veins. At rest, the long, slender wings are held rooflike over the body. They usually become active at dusk or in the evening and are sometimes attracted to lights.

To see a doodlebug, take a spoon and gently scoop out the sand from the bottom of a pit. Their well-camouflaged bodies are easy to miss when they are not moving. I always like to hedge my bet by running the sand through a small kitchen strainer. Have a small hand lens at the ready, since most species are only about ¼ of an inch or less in length. I plan to create my own sandy habitat for doodlebugs this spring in a corner of my insect garden. This way I can catch these pit builders and ambush artists in action right here at home. Hopefully the neighborhood cats won't think that I have created an outdoor sandbox for their convenience.

Daddy Longlegs

Walk along any moist, shady path and you will see them, clambering over the ground by the dozens. You may find them scavenging such diverse delicacies as dead insects, fungus, abandoned crackers, even bird droppings. Some species congregate en masse with legs intertwined in protected places on buildings or under bridges in the fall and winter, resembling a nightmarish hairball. In spite of their eight-legged countenance, they are not spiders at all, nor are they venomous. In fact, they lack fangs altogether and do not bite. They are the daddy longlegs, or harvestmen, a subset of arachnids distantly related to spiders. More than five thousand species of daddy longlegs live in both temperate and tropical regions of the world, many of which have yet to be studied or catalogued by scientists.

About two hundred species of daddy longlegs are known to inhabit North America, including several species introduced from Europe. Daddy longlegs are primarily nocturnal but may be abundant during the day on the floor of shaded woods, resting on tree trunks, or basking on leaves. Several species prefer to live in caves.

Although often confused with spiders, daddy longlegs are classified in a different subset of arachnids. Unlike spiders, the head, chest, and abdomen of daddy longlegs are broadly fused into what appears to be only one body region, not two. This body plan, coupled with their inability to produce silk, easily distinguishes daddy longlegs from their equally leggy look-alike, the cellar spiders. Also called daddy longlegs, cellar spiders are commonly encountered in and around our homes, where they are rarely found away from their seemingly messy webs.

In 1658, Thomas Mouffet, whose daughter Patience is thought by some scholars to have inspired the popular nursery rhyme "Little Miss Muffet," wrote of daddy longlegs in his book *Theatre of Insects* and called them shepherd spiders. In fact, the order of arachnids in which daddy longlegs are placed, Opiliones, is derived from the Latin word *opilio*, meaning shepherd. Their long legs suggest the curious technique of some European shepherds who walked about on stilts to keep an eye on their flocks. Robert Hooke mentions shepherd spiders in his book *Micrographia*, published in 1665. Hooke recalled an ancient English superstition that anyone who intentionally kills a shepherd spider will have bad luck. Later, English farmers who frequently saw them walking through their gardens and fields, especially during the fall harvest period, dubbed them "harvestmen."

Most North American harvestmen are rather drab brown or dull gray in color, although a few are rusty red or brightly mottled in black and white. One common species even has a sporty stripe running the length of its back. The average body length of harvestmen may reach nearly ½ inch, although some tropical giants may approach 1 inch with legs exceeding 6 inches! Other species of harvestmen have short legs and are mitelike in appearance, with bodies never exceeding ½₀ of an inch in length.

The front of the body, which bears the eyes, mouth, and legs, is broadly joined to a short abdomen, giving the impression of a single body region. Some cave-dwelling species are blind, while others have two eyes set on a raised, turretlike bump on the head. The mouthparts consist of a pair of pincerlike chelicerae and leglike pedipalps.

Harvestman scavenge upon dead insects, plants, fungus, fruit, and plant sap and prey upon small insects and other invertebrates. Most predatory species attack small insects, while others are specialists, preferring to dine on other invertebrates, such as snails. Food is seized by the pedipalps, passed to the chelicerae for crushing, and then pushed into the mouth. Unlike other arachnids that must liquefy their food before eating it, harvestmen are able to ingest small particles of solid food.

Harvestmen seem to defy gravity. Impossibly thin, nearly invisible legs support their small, round bodies. Their legs may exceed their body length many times. And the feet of harvestman are constructed of numerous minute segments, affording them great flexibility. The long, second pair of legs is extremely sensitive to touch and functions much like the antennae of insects. Harvestmen will gently comb the ground in front of them with these sensitive structures as they search for food. Although usually quite slow as they move about the forest floor, harvestmen can move quickly when threatened.

While delicate, harvestmen are hardly defenseless. Located between the base of the first and second pairs of legs on each side are the openings to a repugnatorial scent gland. The secretions emitted by these glands contain quinones and phenols, giving the animal an acrid odor and repelling even the most aggressive of predators. Some harvestmen spray this noxious mixture at potential enemies, while others combine it with saliva, spread it on one or more appendages, and thrust the mixture at their attackers.

It is not uncommon to find harvestman traveling on less than their full complement of eight legs. Self-amputation is also an important means of defense. Nerve impulses generated within the discarded legs cause muscles to alternately contract and relax. The separated limb continues to twitch for up to an hour after it has become detached. It is hypothesized that the continued flexing of the leg will distract predators and give the harvestman an opportunity to escape. Although a novel means of defense, it is a method of diminishing returns since the legs cannot be regenerated.

Unlike all but the most primitive of spiders, harvestmen have segmented abdomens. The genital opening is located beneath the abdomen, near the center of the body. A pair of spiracles, or breathing holes, are located the second segment of the abdomen. Active species, such as our Virginia harvestmen, may possess additional spiracles on their legs.

Courtship among most harvestmen is nonexistent, although rival males may battle with one another over receptive females. Unlike spiders, harvestmen engage in direct copulation. Facing the female, the male extends his reproductive organ toward the female's genital opening. She may even guide him with her chelicerae. As they mate, the couple will gently stroke each other with their long legs. Some males may remain with the female after copulation to guard her while she lays her eggs. Parthenogenesis is known in some species of daddy longlegs, a phenomenon where females reproduce without first mating with a male.

At least one species of North American harvestman meets in leks, or courting grounds. Damp clumps of moss or rotting logs and stumps may serve as both pick-up spots and nurseries. Males will begin fighting with one another when females are present, clamping their chelicerae on each other's legs in an attempt to pull them off. The victorious male will then copulate repeatedly with the female over the next few hours.

Shortly after mating, the female seeks a damp location to deposit her eggs. Moist humus, moss, rotten wood or snail shells are all suitable sites. The female ovipositor of some species consists of reinforced rings connected by thin extensive membranes and housed within a protective sheath. At the time of egg laying, the entire structure can be extended at a considerable distance from the genital opening. Female harvestman may lay several batches in their lifetime, with hundreds of eggs in each batch. In a few species of harvestmen, the female will carefully guard her clutch of eggs, but in most species the female simply walks away, never to see her young.

A South American species of daddy longlegs is the only known arachnid that exhibits parental care. Males construct a nest from flakes of bark and mud. A female will court several males in her nest before mating. In this mating system, it is the male daddy longlegs that carefully selects a mate. Assured of his paternity, the male will guard the eggs for a few days even after they hatch. But he does not feed them, and soon the young will disperse.

All too often the victims of our unwarranted antipathy, harvestmen deserve to take their rightful place among the other fascinating animals of this world. Take a moment to observe a harvestman as it quietly ambles across your path or nibbles on a bit of fungus. Little is known of their lifestyles and preferences, and a keen observer can offer new insights into their secretive lives.

Dazzling Dragons
and Damsels

The next time you see someone out in the field with binoculars, don't assume they are simply bird-watching. They could be dragonfly-watchers! Insect-watching, with the aid of binoculars, is rapidly becoming a popular pastime among birders, entomologists, and other naturalists. Butterflies led the movement a few years ago, but now dragonfly- and damselfly-watching is quickly catching on. Why? Because unlike most insects, many butterflies, dragonflies, and damselflies can be reliably identified by sight alone. As in the birding world, a multitude of field guides, regional lists, and Web sites are at the disposal of dragonfly-watchers throughout the world.

Dragonflies and damselflies together make up the insect order Odonata, a term derived from the Greek word *odon,* meaning "toothed." The jaws of adult odonates are equipped with a battery of teeth or spines for macerating mosquitoes, gnats, midges, and the other small airborne insects they use as food. They locate their prey with the aid of two large compound eyes, each with 10,000 to 30,000 individual lenses, giving them a nearly 360-degree view of the world. In addition to wings, the thorax bears three pairs of spiny legs used rarely for walking, but instead to form a basket to scoop up their prey on the wing. One species of dragonfly has been recorded to capture and consume three hundred mosquitoes in one day.

Odonates possess four elongate, sometimes brightly colored, wings, each with an intricate network of supporting veins. Up to one-third or more of their body mass is dedicated to powerful flight muscles that can generate up to fifty wing beats per second. Unlike many four-winged insects, odonate fore- and hind wings do not necessarily function in concert with one another. As they accelerate, the fore- and hind wings begin to beat in unison, but in slower flight each pair of wings operates independently.

Dragonflies are among the world's most agile aerialists. Just try to catch one on the wing! Some species have been clocked at speeds up to thirty-five miles per hour. They can hover effortlessly, or fly short distances backwards. Their bristly antennae and wing hairs determine changes in wind speed and direction. The U.S. Navy and Air Force have studied their aerial acrobatics in wind tunnels and have learned that, among other things, dragonflies twist their wings on the downstroke, creating miniature whirlwinds to reduce the air pressure above the wing to create lift.

The largest dragonfly wingspan ever is 28 inches, known from the fossil record dating back nearly 250 million years. Today, the world's largest living odonate is a Central and South American species of damselfly with a 7½-inch wingspan. The largest known dragonfly in the United States lives in the Southwest and has a wingspan in excess of 3 inches, although it appears to be much larger as it darts about in pursuit of hapless insect prey.

The long, slender abdomen, particularly of dragonflies, has inspired a folk mythology resulting in several colorful monikers. "Devil's darning needles" were thought to sew together the lips of wicked children as they slept. Other names such as "horse stingers," "eye stickers," and "mule killers" suggest our preoccupation with the long and seemingly menacing abdomen of dragonflies, when in fact they are harmless. The "mosquito hawk" is the most appropriate colloquialism, clearly indicating their predilection for preying upon certain insect pests, both as adults and as larvae.

Dragonflies and damselflies are easily distinguished from one another. Dragonflies are generally larger and stouter than damselflies. Their hemispherical eyes are so large they often meet at the top of their head. Damselfly eyes are bulging, yet proportionally smaller, never touching, giving their head somewhat of a barbell shape. Dragonflies always perch with their wings spread apart, while damselflies usually hold their wings together above the body when at rest. The exceptions to this rule are the damselflies known as spreadwings, who keep their wings outspread when at a rest.

Dragonflies and damselflies, part and parcel of summer, are most often seen in flight on warm sunny days near bodies of freshwater. In Virginia, more than 170 species of dragonflies and damselflies may be observed from April through November. The dedicated dragonfly-watcher surveying marshes, swamps, fens, bogs, seeps, and other habitats near streams, rivers, and lakes will encounter a diverse assortment of species such as the white-tailed skimmer, ebony jewelwing, American ruby spot, green darner, blue dasher, widow, dwarf skimmer, southern sprite, and seepage dancer.

Males of the larger dragonfly species patrol set territories along the water's edge, driving off rival suitors. The size of the territory is often proportional to the size of the dragonfly; larger species generally have larger territories. Territories vary from one to ten feet in width. The length of the territory is determined by the male's visual acuity; some species are able to detect motion as far away as thirty feet. Females entering the territory are quickly approached as potential mates, while males and other insects are aggressively driven away.

Odonates are peculiar among insects with regard to the location of their copulatory organs. Before mating, the male dragonfly must transfer sperm from the genital opening located at the tip of his abdomen to a special sexual organ located near the thorax. Like a contortionist, the male bends the tip his abdomen downward and forward until it comes into contact with the sperm storage organ. Once his organ is charged with sperm, the male alights just ahead of the female. He reaches behind her head with special claspers at the tip of his abdomen and grasps her slender neck (damselflies) or head (dragonflies). He lifts off with his mate in tow. She too shares in the effort, like a cyclist in tandem. On the wing, she initiates the "flying-wheel" position by curving her abdomen downward and forward until it comes into contact with the male's sexual organ.

In some species of dragonflies, the fertilized female will lay eggs while still in tandem. Depending upon the habits of her species, she carefully inserts her eggs with the tip of her abdomen into the tissues of aquatic plants, buries them in mud or sand, or releases them directly into the water, sometimes broadcasting them from high above. Eggs are usually laid singly or in small groups to ensure that the young larvae will not have to compete with each other for food, increasing their chances for survival.

The more delicately built damselflies are so adept at airborne couplings that they can simultaneously hover over a stem, each nibbling on aphids like so many berries on a vine. As he inseminates the female, the male simultaneously scrapes out the sperm of her previous mate. He then stays with the female through the egg-laying process to defend his reproductive investment and assure that he alone is the father of her offspring. The female damselfly carefully lays her eggs inside the tissues of submerged plants. She accomplishes this task by completely submerging herself underwater with the male still in tandem. Much of his body remains above water. Afterwards he may assist his mate by attempting to fly to help pull her back to the surface.

The length of time from egg to adult varies among odonates according to species and circumstances. Some species complete their life cycle within a month, while others require five or six years to reach maturity. Several species have adapted to drought conditions by suspending all activity, thereby lengthening the normal time of development indefinitely.

Most odonates spend the bulk of their time in water as larvae. However, the larvae of some tropical species inhabit the moist leaf litter on the forest floor. Still others live in small isolated accumulations of water found in the axils of bromeliad plants that festoon the trunks and branches of trees high off the ground. Some North American dragonfly larvae construct tunnels in muddy bogs, emerging at night to hunt for insects and spiders.

Odonates undergo incomplete metamorphosis, where the aquatic larvae resemble the terrestrial adults, lacking only developed wings. Like the adults, larval odonates are voracious predators. Their elongate lower lip, or labium, is hinged at its base and can be extended like an arm. At the end of the lip are two jawlike structures armed with sharp teeth. To capture prey, the young odonate thrusts its prehensile labium forward with lightning speed, seizing insects, worms, and occasionally small fish up to one inch away. When not in use, the labium is folded underneath the body of the odonate with the jawlike structures covering the lower part of its face like a hockey mask.

Like many aquatic animals, odonate larvae extract oxygen directly from the water. Dragonfly larvae have tracheal gills in the walls of their rectum. Water is alternately drawn in and forced out of the anus, not only to breathe but also to quickly propel them through the water. Since dragonfly larvae use stealth to capture their prey, this jet propulsion system serves as a method of escaping from predators. Damselfly larvae have three leaflike tracheal gills attached to the very tip of the abdomen.

The mature odonate larva usually leaves the water at night to crawl up on an emergent plants or rocks on shore. Its old skin, or exuviae, splits along predetermined lines of weakness, allowing the newly formed adult to escape. By morning the odonate is ready to take flight. For several days, the soft, pale body of the newly emerged adult is especially vulnerable to predation by birds or other odonates.

For centuries, dragonflies have fascinated the Japanese and have been depicted in both modern and ancient arts and crafts. In ancient times, Japan was called *Akitsu shima,* which means "dragonfly island." The ubiquitous rice fields no doubt kept odonates and the Japanese people in close proximity to one another. Young boys would tie weights to the end of a piece of string and toss it into the air where it would sometimes entangle a dragonfly, or *tombo,* who had mistaken the device for a flying insect.

In recognition of the cultural and environmental value of odonates, the Japanese have created twenty dragonfly sanctuaries. The Dragonfly Park at Ikeda-dani is located in a narrow valley of fifty hectares and supports sixty-eight species of odonates. Images of dragonflies are found throughout nearby Nakamura City, adorning tunnels, sidewalks and city buildings. The Yamma Bashi, or large dragonfly bridge, spans the nearby Ikeda River and is supported by giant sculptures of dragonflies. Even the public transportation system pays tribute to the odonates. The Tosa Kuroshio Train, or Red Dragonfly, links Nakamura City to nearby Kubokawacho.

On a practical level, odonates not only consume vast quantities of mosquitoes and other pestiferous insects, they also serve as important biological indicators of environmental health conditions. Their study and conservation can lead to an empathy that is essential to the preservation of all biological diversity.

The most significant threat to dragonflies and damselflies is the loss or degradation of their aquatic habitats. Only by protecting the bogs, ponds, seepages, streams, and rivers in which they breed and develop can we conserve odonate populations on public and private lands. Dragonfly gardeners can dig ponds in their yards and fields to attract them. Habitats set aside as dragonfly preserves create valuable oases suitable for both environmental education and animal research.

Visit the Odonata Information Network at http://www.iodonata .net/.

Katydid, or Did She?

While winding my way through Richmond's Bryan Park to negoti-
ate the tangle of branches and twisted trunks left in the wake of
Hurricane Isabel, I suddenly came upon the true katydid quietly
sitting on an oak stump. The body of the leafy green insect was
nearly two inches long and almost entirely enveloped in remarkably leaflike wings. She had wedged her scimitarlike egg-laying
tube, or ovipositor, into the soft, water-soaked wood. There, her
eggs would be protected from the wind, rain, and cold, and hatch
the following spring into green, wingless, and leggy nymphs.

Both true katydid adults and nymphs feed on the leaves of a
broad range of deciduous trees, especially oaks. Yet, in spite of their
leafy diet, these intriguing animals are not pests, and their presence
should never be cause for alarm. From July through October, the
evening calls of true katydids are the loudest and most familiar in
eastern North America. Males produce calls to attract females as
mates or in response to the calls of other katydid species by rubbing
the bases of their forewings together. Filelike pegs on one wing are
rubbed against a scraperlike ridge on the other to produce their call.
These amorous scrapings have been variously described as "harsh"
or "noisy." To my ear, their calls are extremely pleasing, resembling
the guiro, or *rascador,* a Latin percussion instrument consisting of
a dry, ribbed gourd that is scraped with a stick.

Unlike most katydids and crickets, true katydid females also
possess sound-producing organs and are capable of responding
to calling males. When either the male or female is threatened, it
rasps loudly and raises its oval forewings in a bluff that increases
its overall size and creates a more fearsome appearance. Both male
and female katydids hear these and other calls with their tympana,
earlike organs located on the shins of their front legs.

True katydids range from eastern Colorado, Ontario, and Massachusetts southward to Texas and Florida. In the northern part
of their range, the male's call consists of two to five pulses per
second, while their southern counterparts have a faster call consisting of up to a dozen pulses per second.

The common name "katydid" is onomatopoeic, suggested by the male's call, which has been variously described as "katy-did, she did" or "katy-did, she didn't." Their scientific name, *Pterophylla* (wing leaf) *camellifolia* (tea leaf) was clearly inspired by their wonderfully leafy appearance. But, in spite of their well-developed leaflike wings, true katydids cannot fly. Instead they can glide downwards to a lower perch among the branches, but later must crawl back up to get to a higher perch.

Katydids are regularly preyed upon by birds, bats, spiders, frogs, snakes, and other insect-eaters. House cats frequently take a toll on these insects, often presenting their owners with the dubious gift of a mortally wounded or dead katydid.

At one time, Virginia legend held that a katydid in the house predicted the arrival of unexpected visitors. People also believed that a katydid calling inside the house was a sign that a member of the family had the gift of music. Today, upon hearing their soothing calls on a summer night emanating from the trees in my neighborhood, I am simultaneously filled with sense of wonder, well-being, and hope.

To see pictures of different kinds of katydids and listen to their calls, visit http://natl.ifas.ufl.edu/katydid.htm.

A "Bug Zapper Bites Man" Story

I liken the snap and crackle of a bug zapper frying its hapless victims on a warm summer evening to the shrill scraping of nails on a chalkboard. These indiscriminate electrocution devices needlessly lure countless night-flying insects to their untimely deaths with the same eerie purple light used to illuminate psychedelic posters and discos. The magnitude of the carnage is staggering. Americans buy approximately a million bug zappers annually thinking they are killing mosquitoes. The number of units has no doubt increased with concerns over diseases like West Nile virus. Yet studies show that 95 percent of the insect species killed are nonbiting, mostly beneficial insects.

Researchers estimate that from 71 billion to 350 billion beneficial insects—pollinators and insect predators among them—are killed annually by bug zappers in the United States. Moths, an important component of the pollinator nightshift, are especially hard hit. One study showed that 250 mosquito predators were killed for every single mosquito dispatched.

In another study, nearly half of the victims were caddisflies and midges. To most people, nonbiting midges closely resemble their bloodthirsty, disease-spreading cousins, but they lack the syringe-like mouthparts to bite and deliver pathogens. Diminishing midge populations night after night take food away from the frogs, fish, lizards, birds, and bats that also prey on mosquitoes and their larvae.

The truth is that in terms of attractiveness to mosquitoes, bug zappers simply can't compete with humans. Given a choice, a hungry female mosquito will always be drawn to the body heat and carbon dioxide given off by a human host over the cold, bluish glow of the bug zapper. Bug zapper manufacturers aren't pulling a fast one. They simply claim that their devices kill insects, including mosquitoes. A New Jersey entomologist and high school student collected and identified the kill from zappers at six sites over the course of a summer and found that nearly fourteen thousand insects were killed. Of these, only thirty-one were mosquitoes and other biting insects.

Even bug zappers spiced up with chemical attractants, such as carbon dioxide or octenol, are ineffective. Sonic and ultrasonic devices don't work either. If local, state, and federal agencies, with years of experience in mosquito control to their credit, don't use these devices to control mosquitoes, why should you?

The best method for reducing local mosquito populations is to eliminate standing water found in clogged gutters, planters, birdbaths, tree holes, stumps, and other unnecessary water containers. Stock your garden and fishponds with mosquito fish. Stay indoors during peak mosquito activity periods (mornings, dusk, and early evening). When working outdoors, use repellents with DEET and wear protective clothing.

I recently shared some of this information with a shopper on the way to the checkout line at the hardware store. Rising out of her shopping cart was a brand-new bug zapper, nestled on a bed of repellents, candles, creams, and oils. At the end of our conversation she stopped, thanked me, and returned the useless device to the shelf, saving seventy-five dollars in the process. One down, 999,999 consumers to go.

Dog-days Are Here Again!

A sudden burst of "song" punctuates the air in Virginia's parks and neighborhoods. Likened by some to the sound of a buzz saw chewing through a board, it's actually the mating call of the male dog-day harvestfly, or cicada. Their raucous chorus heralds the beginning of the summer's heat in late June or early July. This annual ritual takes place in the regions of coniferous and mixed hardwood forests throughout the northeastern United States and adjacent Canada.

The black body of the dog-day cicada, trimmed with green markings on its head and thorax, measures just over one inch in length. The membranous wings span more than three inches, supported by a spare network of black and green veins. The two upper angles of a triangular-shaped head are fitted with bulging, but not particularly large, green compound eyes. Nestled between them are three simple eyes to detect light and dark. Below, a large bulging facial plate strengthened by distinct cross braces houses a powerful internal sucking apparatus. Short, sharp beaks, found in all cicadas and their relatives, including aphids, mealy bugs, and plant hoppers, are used to pierce plant tissues and pump out sap. Two types of saliva aid these animals in their sap-feeding activities. The first type is injected into the plant, forming a hardened sheath to accommodate their short, strawlike mouthparts, while the second functions as an anticoagulant, breaking down starches and cell walls to maintain the free flow of sap.

Females lay their eggs in slits cut into stems of trees and shrubs with their large, razorlike egg-laying apparatus. The emerging nymphs fall to the ground, digging into the soil with well-developed front legs. As with the adults, cicada nymphs use piercing-sucking mouthparts to tap into the roots of plants and imbibe sap. Cicadas undergo incomplete metamorphosis. Unlike the complete metamorphosis of butterflies and moths, whose young never look like their parents, the nymphs of cicadas resemble wingless adults. Depending upon conditions, the nymphal stage lasts two to five years. This overlapping of generations ensures adult emergence every year.

After sundown, the mature nymph prepares to forever leave the safety of its subterranean life. Breaking through the surface of the soil, the nymph quietly and steadfastly crawls upward on the vertical surfaces offered by trees, walls, and fences. Gripping the surface firmly with their claws, the nymph begins its final molt. Its back splits open along predisposed lines of weakness, revealing a new pale green and white insect with only crumpled green pads for wings. Within thirty minutes, the wings of the newly emerged adult are fully formed, although it will be several hours before its body is strong and hard enough for a first flight. The most familiar element of this amazing late-night transformation remains behind for all to see: the shed skin, or exuviae. The exuviae is a hollow and exact replica of the nymph, complete in the smallest detail. Here you can clearly see that the forelegs of cicada nymphs are remarkably adapted for a life of digging underground.

Cicadas are best known for the shrill calls of the male, which are often audible over considerable distances. Two special organs located at the base of the abdomen produce the song. Each organ is covered with a thin membrane attached to powerful muscles. Driven by the contraction and relaxation of this muscle, the membrane buckles and snaps back into place in quick succession to create a series of clicks or buzzes, hundreds of times per second. The resultant song is amplified by hollow chambers located immediately adjacent to the sound-producing organs. With rhythmic movements of the abdomen, the male cicada can modulate the quality and intensity of the call simply by opening or closing the sound-producing organs. Each species of cicada has a distinctively shaped instrument to produce its own unique call.

Throughout history, humans around the world have prized cicadas for their spiritual, medicinal, and nutritional value. In both Oriental and Greek mythology, cicadas symbolize sun gods, a result of their preference for hot, sunny locales. Deification of the cicada is seen in Greek jewelry and Pompeian mosaics. The Chinese carved jade cicadas as funeral offerings, placing them on the deceased's tongue. In central Australia, cicadas, or wutnimmera, are symbolized as totems. The ancient Greeks attributed curative powers to cicadas, roasting and consuming them for the treatment of bladder pains. Several tribes of Native Americans recognized cicadas as a nutritional food source and eagerly consumed them. Today in Shanghai, cicadas are boiled in a concoction of anise, mashed garlic, assorted vegetables, and rice wine before being deep-fried, skewered with bamboo picks, and served as a delicacy.

My interest in cicadas is on another level. Aside from their intrinsic biological value, I regard cicadas as old friends who reappear year after year. For untold millennia, their ancient mating calls have marked the transition of the seasons around the world. I have no doubt that, as with every year, their summer song will end all too soon, ushering in yet another autumn, harbinger of an all-too-quiet winter.

What's in a Word?

The mispronunciation of words in everyday conversation is common and forgivable, although I do wince when world leaders consistently mispronounce "nuclear." But I do take exception to the constant misuse of words such as "symbiosis." Symbiosis is often used to denote a positive, mutually satisfying relationship between a company and its customers. Even an online version of the *Oxford English Dictionary* supports this positive notion of symbiosis, defining it as "mutually advantageous connection between people."

Now, I am not a grammarian and am hardly in a position to quibble with the *OED*, but to a biologist, this is not what symbiosis means. The word is derived from the Greek words *syn,* meaning with or together, and *biosis,* or manner of life. Notice there is no judgment, implied or otherwise, as to the nature of that relationship. Instead, there are other perfectly useful words that convey the nature of a symbiotic relationship, good, bad, or indifferent, among all kinds of organisms.

"Mutualism" is usually the word we are looking for, and its meaning is quickly apparent. Derived from the Latin *mutuarius,* meaning reciprocal, mutualism clearly implies that both partners benefit from the relationship. For example, Costa Rican acacia ants have a mutualistic relationship with acacias. The ants live only in the swollen and hollow thorns of a certain species of acacia. They are very territorial and regularly patrol the nest-plant. Agitated workers release an alarm pheromone, a chemical call to arms, that brings their sisters boiling out of their thorn hideaways to drive off hapless plant-feeders, beasts and bugs alike. In addition to shelter, the acacias provide their defenders with nectar and protein via specialized structures.

Commensalism is a symbiotic relationship between two species in which one benefits and the other is not adversely affected. Some tiny flies depend on the predigested body fluids sloshing about in the prey of spiders. They have even been known to use the relatively broad expanse of the spider's back as a staging area where they grooming themselves as they wait for the next victim. Usually, the spider and the flies live in harmony. However, the sheer volume of the victim's fluids imbibed by high numbers of flies lining up to feed may smack of parasitism as far as a hungry spider is concerned.

Another type of symbiosis is parasitism. Both the Greek *parasitos* and the Latin *parasitus* refer to those eating at the table of another, either as guests or spongers. Parasites are intimately involved with one or more hosts, either internally or externally, usually as spongers. Some parasites (lice) are completely dependent on their hosts for their development, while others (fleas and mosquitoes) visit their hosts only briefly. Because of their dependence, parasites may weaken but seldom kill their hosts directly.

However, parasitoids, such as wasps used as biological controls in agriculture, behave as borderline parasites and predators. The larvae of these transient parasites feed internally on the tissues of live caterpillars, eventually causing their death.

Thanks to Virginia's Standards of Learning, today's middle-school students will be able to use the word "symbiosis" properly. Soon they will take their places in the workforce and bring corporate America up to speed.

The Eyes Have It

This past summer, I happened upon a dog-day cicada sitting quietly on a tree trunk. It had apparently transformed the previous night before from a chunky, subterranean larva to a much more elegant and winged adult. Its greenish body, flecked with gold, almost shimmered in the early-morning sun.

What struck me most about this handsome animal were its eyes. They bulged off the corners of its triangular head as if they were about to burst. Set between these unblinking, greenish orbs was a triad of much smaller eyes. How I must have looked to this creature with five eyes!

The cicada is equipped with the two basic types of insect eyes: compound and simple. Compound eyes are found in most adults and larvae that develop by gradual metamorphosis (e.g., dragonflies, true bugs, grasshoppers). The surface of each compound eye consists of multiple facets, or lenses. In species with large numbers of lenses, each facet is hexagonal in shape, maximizing the number of lenses per surface area. Compound eyes have hundreds, even thousands of lenses, with some dragonflies having as many as thirty thousand in each eye.

Optically, there are two different kinds of compound eyes. Each lens of day-active insects picks up just part of the whole scene. Their brain interprets the world as a field of pixels, with each dot varying in brightness. In nocturnal species, the lenses work more as one to maximize the amount of light available and form a fuzzy, single image for their brain to sort out.

Whether intended for day- or nighttime use, the tiny lenses of insect eyes are limited in their visual acuity because of diffraction, the blurriness inherent around the edges of the lenses. Even the best insect eyes probably view a scene as if it were knitted in the coarsest of wool yarn and viewed at a distance of about a foot away. For a honeybee to see as clearly as a human, each eye would have to be three feet across!

Most insects do not see the color red, but they do see blue, green, orange, and yellow. Many use polarized light to orient themselves, especially those species that must return to a nest. Others are capable of detecting ultraviolet light (UV), which is invisible to humans. Many flowers have petals marked with UV nectar guides that attract and direct insects to the pollen- and nectar-laden centers.

Some species have compound eyes with zones of acuity, usually forward and upward, to help them hone in on specific kinds of action. In some insects, this specialization is found only in males to help them find in a mate. Both male and female predators have acute zones related to prey capture. The wide-set eyes of mantids give them the added benefit of binocular vision and, as a result, depth perception. Depth perception is critical to all predators because it gives them the ability to gauge whether or not prey is within striking distance.

Night-flying species get around by maintaining a constant angle with distant sources of light, such as the stars and moon. If they choose a nearby source, such as a porch light, they must enter into a pattern of ever-smaller spirals until they arrive at the light. Bathed in "daylight," they shift out of their nighttime activity mode and shut down.

Day or night, the real function of compound eyes may be to detect movement as perceived by rapid changes in light intensity. Fast-flying diurnal insects are better able to process a quick succession of flickering images to produce a clearer image of their surroundings than their slow- or night-flying counterparts.

Many flying insects have both compound and simple eyes. Each simple eye, or ocellus, has only one lens. The ocelli are located on the top of the head and are better suited for detecting light and dark than they are for forming images. They are more sensitive than compound eyes at low light levels. The ocelli help to regulate the insect's daily rhythms related to light intensity. In flying insects, they are used to perceive the overall distribution of light to help maintain equilibrium in the air.

Beetle grubs, caterpillars, maggots, and other larvae that undergo complete metamorphosis have clusters of simple eyes called stemmata. They are capable of minimal image reception, probably seeing the world only as large areas of light and dark. The stemmata are greatly reduced or absent in parasites or species living in total darkness deep in the soil or inside caves.

Given that the development of simple eyes might have led to an optically superior system similar to our own, it is curious that nature has invested so much in compound eyes. Clearly we still have much to learn about the advantages that compound eyes impart to their owners.

One of the reasons that humans tend to dislike most insects is that they are so alien in their appearance, a fact reinforced by their large, unblinking eyes. But it is the large, forward-looking eyes of mantids and jumping spiders that give them some semblance of personality. And with those eyes they seem to respond to us with the same curiosity and wariness that we afford them. Maybe they aren't so alien after all.

Bugs
Matter!

Only a mere fraction of Virginia's insects spread disease, damage crops, or harm forests. Some are absolutely essential for maintaining our quality of life. Insects such as bees, wasps, flies, and some beetles are the primary pollinators of our gardens, orchards, and crops. Predatory species of insects and spiders routinely capture countless numbers of insect pests, reducing our costly and ultimately harmful dependence on pesticides. Still others clean up plant and animal remains, recycling precious nutrients for future use by other organisms. The vast majority of insect species may have little or no direct impact on our lives, but they are all just as fascinating to observe and study!

Insects provide other practical services as well. They react to subtle environmental changes within just weeks, whereas plants and vertebrates may take months, even years to respond. Equipped with a basic understanding of insect ecology, scientists use insects as bioindicators for environmental quality, past and present. Insect remains recovered from archaeological sites provide important clues to determine environmental conditions that prevailed hundreds, even thousands of years ago. Aquatic insects serve as bioindicators in wetland management, revealing subtle changes in water quality caused by contaminants and temperature fluctuation.

Insects at the scene of a homicide may provide important clues to criminal investigators. Forensic specialists use the orderly progression of insect scavengers associated with any remains to determine time and place of death. They can even indicate if the victim had been moved. Civil suits occasionally depend on insect evidence to determine liability for damages caused by costly pest infestations. The predictability of pest life cycles are used to fix the relative time and place of infestation.

Insects are tailor-made for representing many of the biological processes set forth in Virginia's Standards of Learning for the life sciences. They are second to none when it comes to demonstrating life cycles, reproduction, cooperation, competition, and food webs in the classroom. Live insects are readily available, easy to keep and house, and are inexpensive to maintain. The familiar, yet bizarre nature of insects, spiders, and other arthropods makes them the perfect ambassadors for environmental education and awareness.

The study of Virginia's diverse insect fauna will continue to produce important insights into our past, present, and future. Simply taking the time to recognize some of the more common insects that live with us is a sure-fire way to enrich our own lives and is instrumental to the appreciation and conservation of Virginia's natural heritage.

Take a
Pollinator
to Lunch

It's winter. As I look out my window at all of the snow and ice, my mind is naturally drawn to thoughts of—what else?—Spring! We all seem to be drawn to the sudden promise of renewal marked by fresh, leafy growth and flowers bursting from their buds. But we all too often take for granted the animals that make all of this plant life possible, the pollinators. They are critical to the survival of more than 90 percent of the world's flowering plants. And without pollinators, our diets around the globe would consist of bland meals of wind-pollinated grains and very little else.

Pollination is the physical act of moving pollen grains from the male reproductive organs of one flower and depositing them onto the female organs of another in the same species. Incapable of self-fertilization, most flowering plants rely upon pollinators such as birds, bats, and a myriad of insects to carry out this task. But plants are hardly passive in their efforts to distribute pollen. Not just simply organs of reproduction, flowers also function as billboards, enticing hungry pollinators with their flashy colors and intoxicating scents. Flowers offer up to their guests a veritable smorgasbord of high-protein pollen, sweet nectar, and a delectable salad of tender, succulent petals.

Whether they have backbones or not, pollinators all share one thing in common—their bodies are virtual pollen magnets. Whether feathered, furred, or otherwise fuzzy, pollen grains regularly stick to the bodies of pollinators and are dropped off on other blooms as they scramble among the petals and anthers for goodies.

Nearly all of our fruit, nut, and vegetable crops depend on insects for pollination. Without them, there is a drastic reduction in fruit set, which not only impacts our food supply directly, it also limits the seeds available to grow the next season's crops. Some of the better-known crops pollinated by vertebrates include pineapples (birds) and bananas (birds and bats). But insects reign supreme as the most important pollinators in most agricultural systems.

Native bees and thrips are the primary pollinators of sugarcane and peas. Artichoke, potato, and tomato crops depend on native bumblebees. Flies and native bees pollinate coffee, tea, and pepper. And all of you chocoholics out there are beholden to flies for your stash of chocolate bars.

The familiar honeybee, a native of Europe, is an important pollinator of many crops in North America. But some scientists think that with a little help, native species of bees might prove to be even more efficient pollinators of some crops. And there is the suspicion that, in some areas, honeybees have had a negative impact on local populations of native bees, directly affecting the chances for survival of many native plants.

Forty-six years ago, Rachel Carson's *Silent Spring* painted a bleak picture of a spring without the chorus of songbirds or buzzing bees among the blossoms. It became a call to arms, and a new era of environmental protection was born. She also suggested that fruitless falls, autumns without pollination or fruit, would become more commonplace. Since then, farmers and governmental agencies both have taken steps to reduce insecticide use that might kill honeybees in the field and in the hive.

But there is still much work to be done to protect and conserve our native insect pollinators. The clearing of dead limbs and trees, along with the loss of open space, reduces or eliminates nesting and breeding sites for many native species of solitary bees and beetles. Excessive mowing and indiscriminate use of herbicides along roadsides are destroying already fragmented habitats, leaving many native pollinators and the plants that depend on them in a very precarious position. Too many of our suburban areas are awash in sterile seas of mowed grass, dreary hedgerows of exotic shrubs, and medians filled with beds of exotic flowers. All of these habitats are of little or no interest to native pollinators.

We can encourage and conserve Virginia's insect pollinators by continuing to set aside more roadsides for plantings of native flowers. And we can reclaim sterile habitats in neighborhoods by increasing our use of native plants, ultimately creating an ever-expanding patchwork of tiny oases for pollinators.

For information on the use of native plants in garden, land management, conservation, and restoration projects, visit the Virginia Division of Natural Heritage at http://www.dcr.state.va.us/dnh/native.htm.

Additional information can be found at the Virginia Native Plant Society at http://www.vnps.org.

For information on the science of pollinator conservation and related links, visit the Ecological Society of America at http://www.esa.org/ecoservices.

The Xerces Society promotes the conservation of all invertebrates, including pollinators, at http://www.xerces.org/Pollinator_Insect_Conservation/index.htm.

Crayfishes, Crawfishes, and Mudbugs

Crayfish, crawfish, crawdads, or mudbugs—whatever you call them, these lobsterlike denizens of freshwater habitats are bound to make a strong impression. To anglers, they are irresistible to bass, trout, and other fish and make excellent bait. Educators consider these crustaceans highly instructive animals in the classroom and laboratory. Aquarium hobbyists view them as curious and interesting pets. Ecologists use the presence or absence of native crayfish to measure environmental health, but decry the arrival of exotic species as a serious environmental threat. Conservationists recognize the precarious situation of those species living in caves and other sensitive habitats and strive to protect them. Landowners sometimes disparage crayfish because their burrowing activities damage lawns, gardens, and earthen dams.

As for me, they bring to mind a wonderful meal of mudbug gumbo on a hot, sticky August night in New Orleans. They are a popular food item in the South, especially in Louisiana, as well as in France and some other European countries. Crayfish harvested by trappers in the wild or farmed in ponds are destined for the dinner table or the end of a fishhook. In Louisiana alone, over 130,000 acres have been set aside for crayfish farming, producing more than 10 million pounds of red swamp crayfish annually.

Recently, I spotted several turretlike chimneys along the James River. They were built with crouton-sized clumps of mud. These conical mounds, topped by a central round hole measuring one inch across, mark the entrances to retreats dug by burrowing crayfishes. Both males and females dig burrows three or more feet deep. These shelters come in handy, especially when they are molting. As they grow larger, crayfishes must shed their external skeletons and need a place to hide. During this time, they are particularly vulnerable to attack by famished fish, hungry herons, ravenous raccoons, and other predators.

Most species of crayfish breed in the spring and summer, but in warmer years their reproductive activities may carry on into the fall. Beneath the female's abdomen is a set of special appendages that can hold a cluster of up to eight hundred fruitlike eggs until they hatch. During this time, she is delicately referred to as being "in berry." After a few weeks or more, the eggs hatch. The young crayfish resemble adults in miniature and will remain with their mother for a short period. The entire lifespan of most crayfish species is about two years.

Crayfish live mainly in shallow waters of ponds, lakes, and streams. But you probably won't see them in the daylight. They are active at night and remain hidden during the day under rocks, logs, debris, or in their burrows. Their diet consists mostly of living and dead plants, but they also eat insects, worms, and other bottom-feeders. Crayfishes forage slowly and deliberately, but react quickly to danger by swimming away backwards, propelled by powerful flips of their tails.

Believe it or not, North America is the world's hot spot for crayfish. Of the nearly 600 species of these crustaceans known worldwide, more than half live in the United States and Canada. Sadly, about 65 species are endangered, while another 195 are in need of protection. However, of the more than 25 species of crayfishes found in Virginia, only one is currently considered threatened. The biggest threats to crayfish populations are habitat degradation or competition from nonnative species of crayfishes. Nonnative species also threaten other aquatic animals and plants.

According to the *American Heritage* online dictionary, the word "crayfish" can probably trace its etymological roots back to the German word *krebiz*, or "edible crustacean." Later, in Old French, they were called *crevice*. This word was adopted into Middle English sometime in the early fourteenth century as "crevise," and by the mid-sixteenth century, people were more often than not misspelling the last half of the word as "fish." The Anglo-Normans apparently uttered the first half of the word in two different ways, resulting in the two equally acceptable modern English pronunciations, "crayfish" and "crawfish."

To find out more about crayfishes, visit the Crayfish Homepage at http://crayfish.byu.edu/index.htm.

Bugs in Focus:
The Art of Making
Little Things Big

From the small size of insects, we are apt to undervalue their appearance. If we could imagine a male atlas beetle, with its polished bronzed coat of mail, and its vast complex horns, magnified to the size of a horse, or even of a dog, it would be one of the most imposing animals in the world.

—Charles Darwin, *Descent of Man* (1871)

Macrophotography is the art of blending science, technology, lots of patience, and a bit of luck to capture the images of objects at life size or greater on film or disc. Insects, spiders, and their relatives are ideal subjects for this kind of photography because they are virtually everywhere and provide a seemingly endless source of interesting shapes, colors, and behaviors.

My interest in photography was not born from a desire to manipulate light, or a fascination with cameras and other photographic equipment. Instead, it was driven by a simple desire to faithfully record the likenesses of the insects, spiders, and other small animals that crossed my path. As a child, the marvelous photos that graced the slick pages of *National Geographic* from the late 1950s through the early 1970s inspired me. The stunning photography of Paul Zahl, Edward Ross, and Robert Sisson filled my head with images of exotic insects and spiders from around the world.

I have been taking pictures of nature since the sixth grade, and insects and spiders were always my favorite subjects. But these early efforts never resembled what I saw in books and magazines. It wasn't until 1997 that I decided to get serious and learn about macrophotography. I bought a brand new Canon EOS Elan II-e, along with a 100-millimeter macrolens, some flashes, and all the necessary cables and other attachments. Then I purchased a wonderfully instructive book, *How to Photograph Insects and Spiders.* The authors not only suggested specific kinds of equipment and where to purchase them, but also where to put the flash, at what angles, and the settings to use. After shooting a few test rolls of film, I began getting the pictures that I wanted.

Photographing insects and spiders is all about magnification. I depend on my 100-millimeter macrolens as my primary lens. It is designed to get me up close and personal, just an inch or so away from my subject. Some insects are a bit skittish, but with a little practice I can usually get right up to most species and fire off a shot or two before they decide to flee the scene.

I also use a teleconverter between my primary lens and camera. This lens doubles the image size of my subject, making it twice life-size on film. To this I sometimes add up to 50 millimeters of extension tubes. Extension tubes are not lenses. They are simply spacers that increase magnification by increasing the distance between my primary lens and the film in my camera.

Depth of field, or the amount of the picture that is in focus, is always an issue with macrophotography. I use smaller apertures to increase the depth of field. The problem here is that a smaller aperture means less light reaches the film. One solution is to slow the shutter speed to allow more light into the camera. But the challenge here is that longer shutter speeds increase the chances that the subject, camera, or both will move while the shutter is open, blurring the picture.

A tripod will certainly keep the camera steady, and a cable release will allow me to trip the shutter without jarring the camera. This is the rig photographers use to take pictures of dew-covered, dead-still insects. But for me, clunky and heavy tripods are of little use for capturing images of most active, fast-moving insects during the heat of the day.

As far as I am concerned, using flashes is the only real option for capturing quality photographs of insects and spiders. Flash photography allows using small apertures and fast shutter speeds to freeze the action and capture crisp images. And, to make sure the camera is as steady as possible, I use elbow and knee pads. They add comfort and help me to steady the camera as I hunker down in rough terrain to shoot bugs in the act of feeding, grooming, mating, or molting.

I started with one flash, but now I use three. I have a ring flash mounted directly on the end of the barrel of my primary lens. Two additional flashes are mounted on brackets at 40- to 45-degree angles on either side of the primary lens. The two side flashes illuminate both the subject and background, while the ring flash reduces any cross-shadows. The results are very satisfying. The downside of this rig is that it is like carrying a brick.

My aperture is usually set at $f16$ or $f22$. My shutter speed is $1/125$ of a second, the fastest speed I can use that synchronizes my camera with my flashes. I use fine-grained professional slide films with smaller ISO numbers (100 or less). These slower-speed films require slower shutter speeds, larger apertures, or flash for proper exposure. My current favorite is Fuji's Velvia 100, but there are other kinds of film that also produce excellent results.

Composition is important. I try to photograph my subjects sitting close to their backgrounds. Insects and spiders shot on a leaf, flower, or bark usually produce good images with depth and context. If they are perched on the end of a branch or some other situation where the background is far away, the flashes will not properly expose the background without further adjusting the camera's settings. If only the subject is properly exposed, the rest of the scene appears black, as if the photo was taken at night. Sometimes this can have a dramatic, isolating effect. But whenever possible, I like a well-exposed background to give the photograph a bit of ecological context.

I usually try to compose the picture so that the picture frame is filled with my subject. I compose the shot by turning the barrel of the lens so that the insect is just the right size in relation to the rest of the frame. Without turning the lens, I gently rock the camera back and forth until I find the "sweet spot," the place where most of the image has the sharpest possible focus. Then I squeeze the shutter and take the picture. The photograph is always better if the wings, legs, and antennae are all in the same plane of focus, but this is not always possible with decidedly three-dimensional species. No matter what, I always make sure that the eyes are in sharp focus. Images of blurry-eyed animals of any kind seldom hold any interest for the viewer.

Even after the insect is properly focused and positioned in the shot, my eye still darts to all corners of the scene before I trip the shutter. I am searching for distracting bits of leaves, grass, twigs, or other debris. If not caught ahead of time, these distractions will become painfully obvious when my slides come back from the developer. I can't tell you how many otherwise "perfect" shots I have taken that were ruined by an errant blade of grass or a wild hair.

I usually bracket my pictures. I take several shots of the same subject at different exposures above and below the proper exposure indicated my camera's internal meter. This increases my chances of getting an image with the right balance of focus, composition, and exposure.

My photo safaris are undertaken in my own insect garden, botanical gardens, and city parks. Whenever possible, I try to go farther afield and visit state or national parks. Habitats with water and a diversity of plants are the most productive places to find insects and spiders, especially on warm, sunny days. It takes time to develop a search pattern for these animals, so I usually spend a minimum of two or three hours at each locality.

Bees, butterflies, beetles, flies, and wasps often swarm around patches of flowers as if they were a buffet. Wandering along watercourses always produces good shots of dragonflies, damselflies, tiger beetles, wolf spiders, and other arthropods. One of the decided advantages I have as an insect photographer is that I am an entomologist. I have a pretty good idea of when and where my quarry will be out and about.

I shoot lots of film, sometimes as many as eight to ten rolls a day. I still miss shots because of dumb things: wrong settings, camera turned off, no film loaded, etc. Many of my photos go right into the trash because they are not in focus, poorly composed, improperly exposed, or have some distracting element. On a good day I might get four to five shots in a roll of thirty-six exposures that, to my eye, are the perfect meld of light, subject, and composition. After nearly eight years, I am still learning about macro photography. And no, I have not yet gone digital, but I will soon, very soon.

My favorite photographs of insects and spiders are those that both illustrate and tell a story. I think photography has helped to change our perspective of these often-misunderstood animals. As their images become more familiar to us, maybe we can finally begin to accept them as fellow species that share our planet, rather than continue to dismiss them as alien creatures that infest it.

Visit some of my favorite insect photography sites at http://www.bugbios.com/entophiles/; http://www.beautifulbugs.com/; http://www.myrmecos.net/.

Loving Lichens

Lichens are the essence of wildness. To find them in abundance is to find a corner of the universe where the environment is still pure and unspoiled.

—Irwin Brodo, *Lichens of North America* (2001)

Lichens are everywhere, yet they are easily overlooked. They festoon boulders and trunks, appearing as subtle splotches of gray paint, roughened clumps of gray green or shocking splashes of fluorescent yellows, reds, and oranges. They come in a variety of forms, ranging from cobbled crusts, leafy rosettes, or tiny treelike growths. Close up and personal, the colors and textures of some lichens suggest a fantastic landscape from another world.

Even our eleven-year-old son appreciates lichens, especially those on the move. Worn on the backs of larval lacewings, bits of lichen provide these predatory insects with a considerable degree of camouflage as they scour trees and shrubs for insect prey.

Lichens are composite organisms engaged in a mutually beneficial partnership whose members hail from as many as three different kingdoms. Lichen fungi, the dominant partner in any lichen, are incapable of making their own food. Instead, they must rely on algae or cyanobacteria (formerly known as blue-green algae) that manufacture food by using the energy of the sun, a process known as photosynthesis. Some lichen fungi hedge their bets by enlisting the services of both algae and cyanobacteria.

Lichens play a significant role in what is referred to as ecological succession. They convert bare rock and seemingly sterile soils into fertile habitats that can support mosses and other plants, paving the way for successive waves of colonizing animals. They are the linchpins of many food webs that include invertebrates and their predators. For example, small lichen-eating mites and insects are preyed upon by spiders, which are in turn consumed by shrews, which are then snatched up by owls or hawks. Caribou and deer also depend on lichens as food. And many birds and small mammals use lichens as insulation material for their nests. Around the world, people use lichens as food, medicines, dye, even as faux shrubbery in model railroad layouts.

Lichens are also important tools in scientific research. There is a small but dedicated group of researchers who study the nearly four thousand species of lichens known in the United States and Canada. These lichenologists not only study the classification, distribution, and ecology of lichens, they also use them as bioindicators. Lichens serve as an early-warning system for researchers monitoring deteriorating air quality and the environmental health of forests.

Next time you wander outdoors, take a moment to look for lichens clinging to life on bare rocks, dry sands, harsh soils, and dead trees. They tolerate extremes of both temperature and drought and seem to thrive in the most inhospitable places. Lichens are a gentle reminder of the incredible diversity and complexity of Virginia's natural heritage.

For more information on lichens, visit http://www.lichen.com.

Epilogue

A native landscape enters a child's mind through a meld of sensations: the smell of seaweed or hay, the sound of cicadas, the cold grit of stone. It is all heart and magic, confusion rather than order, but the feeling it evokes is wholly satisfying and lasting. Gaining this kind of deep familiarity with a landscape other than your native one is like learning to speak a foreign language. You can't hope for quick or easy fluency. You work from the outside in, by accumulating a vocabulary of observed details. . . . Slowly the strange becomes familiar; the familiar becomes precious.

—Jennifer Ackerman, *Notes from the Shore* (1995)

And so it was and is for me. A native southern Californian transplanted from my long-familiar and sparsely vegetated desert surroundings, I have come to know and embrace the relative lushness of Virginia and the riot of insect life it supports. My education continues; what was once wonderfully strange has now become an integral part of my very being.

Suggested Readings

Akre, R. D., G. S. Paulson, and E. P. Catts. *Insects Did It First.* Fairfield: Galleon Press, 1992.

Allen, T. J., J. P. Brock, and J. Glassberg. *Caterpillars in the Field and Garden: A Field Guide to the Butterfly Caterpillars of North America.* New York: Oxford University Press, 2005.

Berenbaum, M. R. *Bugs in the System.* Reading, Mass.: Addison-Wesley, 1995.

Brodo, I. M., S. D. Sharnoff, and S. Sharnoff. *Lichens of North America.* New Haven: Yale University Press, 2001.

Buchman, S. L., and G. P. Nabhan. *The Forgotten Pollinators.* Washington, D.C.: Island Press, 1996.

Burnett, R. *The Pillbug Project: A Guide to Investigation.* Arlington, Va.: National Science Teachers Association, 1992.

Covell, C., Jr. *A Field Guide to Moths of Eastern North America.* Martinsville: Virginia Museum of Natural History, 2005.

Dunkle, S. *Dragonflies through Binoculars: A Field Guide to the Dragonflies of North America.* New York: Oxford University Press, 2000.

Eisner, T. *For Love of Insects.* Cambridge: Belknap Press of Harvard University Press, 2003.

Eisner, T., M. Eisner, and M. Siegler. *Secret Weapons: Defenses of Insects, Spiders, and Other Many-Legged Creatures.* Cambridge: Belknap Press of Harvard University Press, 2005.

Evans, A. V., and C. L. Bellamy. *An Inordinate Fondness for Beetles.* Berkeley and Los Angeles: University of California Press, 2001.

Grissell, E. *Insects and Gardens.* Portland: Timber Press, 2001.

Gordon, D. G. *The Compleat Cockroach: A Comprehensive Guide to the Most Despised (and Least Understood) Creature on Earth.* Berkeley: Ten Speed Press, 1996.

Gordon, D. G. *The Eat-A-Bug Cookbook: 33 Ways to Cook Grasshoppers, Ants, Water Bugs, Spiders, Centipedes, and Their Kin.* Berkeley: Ten Speed Press, 1998.

Himmelman, J. *Discovering Moths: Nighttime Jewels in Your Own Backyard.* Portland, Me.: Down East Books, 2002.

Holdich, D. M., ed. *Biology of Freshwater Crayfish.* Dubuque: Iowa State University Press, 2002.

Hölldobler, B., and E. O. Wilson. *Journey to the Ants: A Story of Scientific Exploration.* Cambridge: Belknap Press of Harvard University Press, 1994.

Hoyt, E. *The Earth Dwellers: Adventures in the Land of Ants.* New York: Simon and Schuster, 1996.

Klausnitzer, B. *Insects: Their Biology and Cultural History.* New York: Universe Books, 1987.

Klein, H. D., and A. M. Wenner. *Tiny Game Hunting: Environmentally Healthy Ways to Trap and Kill the Pests in Your House and Garden.* Berkeley and Los Angeles: University of California Press, 2001.

Knisley, C. B., and T. D. Schultz. *The Biology of Tiger Beetles and a Guide to the Species of the South Atlantic States.* Special Publication Number 5. Martinsville: Virginia Museum of Natural History, 1997.

Levi, H. W., and L. R. *Spiders and Their Kin: A Golden Guide.* New York: Golden Books, 1990.

Marshall, S. *Insects: Their Natural History and Diversity: With a Photographic Guide to the Insects of Eastern North America.* Buffalo: Firefly Books, 2006.

Terwilliger, K., ed. *Virginia's Endangered Species.* Blacksburg, Va.: McDonald and Woodward, 1991.

Wagner, D. *Caterpillars of Eastern North America.* Princeton: Princeton University Press, 2005.

West, L., and J. Ridl. *How to Photograph Insects and Spiders.* Mechanicsburg, Pa.: Stackpole Books, 1994.

Suggested Web Sites

Bugguide, An Online Field Guide to Insects. http://www.bugguide .net/.

Insect Identification Laboratory at Virginia Tech. http://www.ento .vt.edu/bughunt.

Insect Checklists, Distribution, and Identification Resources. http:// www.npwrc.usgs.gov/resource/taxa_i.htm.

Notes on
the Original
Articles

The essays in this book were originally published, in a slightly different and usually abbreviated form, as a series of newspaper columns and cover stories with color photos in the *Richmond Times-Dispatch*. They appeared sporadically at first, usually on the fifth Thursday of every month in the Health and Science section. Since 2002, What's Bugging You? has become a regular feature on the second Thursday of the month, first in the Health and Science section and later in Explore, where it appears today. The title and date of publication for the original columns and cover stories that appear in this book are listed chronologically below:

"Hardly a Threat, Boxelder Bugs Enjoy Their Season for Activity." Health and Science. June 29, 2000.

"Flight of Fancy: Dragonflies, Damselflies Eat Many Insects, Provide Information on Aquatic Habitats." Health and Science. August 10, 2000.

"That Racket in the Woods Is Sweet Music to Cicadas." Health and Science. August 31, 2000.

"Harvestmen are Scavengers Likely Known to Miss Muffet." Health and Science. September 14, 2000.

"Camel Cricket, Despite Bad Rap, Is Deserving of a Second Look." Health and Science. November 30, 2000.

"Odd Behavior Allows Scientist to Determine Insect's Identity." Health and Science. March 29, 2001.

"Spring Means Carpenter Bees Noisily Looking for Mates, Nests." Health and Science. May 10, 2001.

"On Safari in Bryan Park." Health and Science. May 17, 2001.

"Earwigs Have Gotten a Bum Rap since They Help Get Rid of Pests." Health and Science. July 12, 2001.

"Body Snatching Beetles Clear Death on Behalf of Life." Health and Science. August 30, 2001.

"Webworms on Deciduous Tree in Fall Mainly Aesthetic Problem." September 13, 2001.

"Paper Wasps No Paper Tigers When It Comes to Aggression." Health and Science. October 11, 2001.

"State Insects Provide Insights into Past, Present and Future." Health and Science. December 13, 2001.

"Prehistoric-Looking Animals Are Adapted to Living on Land." Health and Science. February 14, 2002.

"And Along Came a Spider—Conquering His Fear, Finding a Fascination." Health and Science. March 28, 2002.

"Take Time to Look for Lichens, Found on Trees, Rocks, Sands." Health and Science. April 11, 2002.

"Wildlife Oasis. Going on Safari at Three Lakes Park." Health and Science. May 23, 2002.

"Appearance of Tent Caterpillars Isn't Necessarily Cause for Alarm." Health and Science. May 30, 2002.

"Virginia BioBlitz Participants Log 1,377 Species at State Park." Health and Science. July 11, 2002.

"Mud Daubers: Solitary Creatures and Dynamos of Nest Architecture." Health and Science. August 29, 2002.

"Appearance of Large Mantids Marks End of Summer Season." Health and Science. October 10, 2002.

"Devices Do Zap Many Insects, But Hardly Any Are Mosquitoes." Health and Science. November 14, 2002.

"Hints of Life: Dormant Insects Await Spring Signs." Health and Science. December 19, 2002.

"What's in a Word? Lower Life Knows, Not Corporate America." Health and Science. February 13, 2003.

"Mulberry Trees Can Provide Scientific, Historical Lessons." Health and Science. March 13, 2003.

"Bugs on the Water." Health and Science. June 12, 2003.

"BioBlitz: Natural Success." Health and Science. June 12, 2003.

"Longer, Warmer Days Bring out Clouds of Tiger Swallowtails." Health and Science. July 10, 2003.

"Survival Often a Major Struggle for Hapless Hercules Beetle." Health and Science. August 14, 2003.

"Scales on Their Wings." Health and Science. September 11, 2003.

"True Katydid Found Depositing Eggs on Bryan Park Oak Stump." Health and Science. October 9, 2003.

"Butterflies' Winter Spots Are Changing." Health and Science. November 13, 2003.

"Beetles Live in Trees for Winter." Health and Science. December 11, 2003.

"Should You Make Ants Say 'Uncle'?" Health and Science. January 8, 2004.

"Bees Do It, and It's Vital That They Do." Explore. February 12, 2004.

"Creating a Garden to Lure Interesting Insects and Spiders." Explore. March 11, 2004.

"Striking It Rich with Oil Beetles." Explore. April 8, 2004.

"Brood X Returns: 80's Flashback; Cicadas Return by the Millions." Explore. May 13, 2004.

"Before Butterflies Take Flight, Caterpillars Are on the Crawl." Explore. June 10, 2004.

"The Nightshift: They Like the Nightlife; They Like to 'Buggy.'" Explore. July 8, 2004.

"Visiting a Tiny Dweller on the Beach." Explore. August 12, 2004.

"A Close Look at Prey and Predator." Explore. September 19, 2004.

"Daily Rumble of Humble 'Bumbles.'" Explore. October 15, 2004.

"The Real Spin on the Black Widow." Explore. November 11, 2004.

"The Eyes Have It: For Insects, Vision Is a Multifaceted View of Nature." Explore. December 9, 2004.

"Roach 101: A Primer on 'Pests.'" Explore. January 13, 2005.

"Odd Little Doodlebugs Are Fierce Predators." Explore. February 10, 2005.

"Bug Portraits: Spiders, Insects and Kin Are Ready for Their Close-up." Explore. March 10, 2005.

"Question Marks Have the Answer." Explore. April 14, 2005.

"Cray, Craw—A Distinctive Creature by Any Name." Explore. May 12, 2005.

Index